The Illustrated Portrait of
SUFFOLK

Overleaf: The Water Jump at Kersey

ALLAN JOBSON

The Illustrated Portrait of
SUFFOLK

ROBERT HALE
LONDON

© Allan Jobson 1973
© Hubert Jobson 1987
First published in Great Britain 1973
Reprinted 1979
New illustrated edition 1987

ISBN 0 7090 3017 7

Robert Hale Limited
Clerkenwell House
Clerkenwell Green
London ECIR OHT

British Library Cataloguing in Publication Data
Jobson, Allan
  The illustrated portrait of Suffolk.—New ed.
  1. Suffolk—Description and travel
  I. Title   II. Jobson, Allan. Portrait of Suffolk
914.26′404858   DA670.S9

Printed in Great Britain by
St. Edmundsbury Press Limited, Bury St. Edmunds, Suffolk
Bound by WBC Bookbinders Limited

Contents

Line Drawings

by Richard S. Taylor

Plates

Credits

To Veronica and Gerald

For thilke ground, that bears the weedes wick
Beares eke the wholesome herbes, and full oft
Next to the foule nettle, rough and thick,
The lily waxeth, white and smooth, and soft;
And next the valley is the hill aloft,
And next the darke night is the glad morrow,
And also joy is next the fine of sorrow.
Chaucer

Reviser's Note

Allan Jobson was a Suffolk man, who had imbibed the county from his earliest years. These dated to well before the Great War. Born in 1889, Allan saw a world far removed from the Suffolk of today or even that of 1972 when he wrote the original *Portrait of Suffolk*.

In revising the book for a new edition in 1987, I have retained the basic text Mr Jobson wrote. The account of agriculture in chapter 8 will always remind me of the county I traversed as a child when the horse still pulled the plough. Minor corrections have been made in chapters 2 to 10 and, as a prospect of the unitary country, chapter 11 of the original *Portrait of Suffolk* has been retained. A postscript has been added to suggest how far the changes foreseen have been effected. More extensive revisions have been made to chapter 1: the reviser is an archaeologist by training.

As a new edition of *Portrait of Suffolk*, this *Illustrated Portrait of Suffolk* with new line drawings by Richard S. Taylor can only serve as a fitting memorial to Allan who died, much respected, at the age of ninety on 27 March 1980.

D. H. Kennett
January 1987

Foreword

A Suffolk Portrait takes more than one sitting. The face like a piece of enamel is clear amongst the shadows of the background. But perhaps, the most expression is to be seen in the hands. The hands that have fashioned so much, so strong and yet so delicate and caressing. The two are not quite equal, the left being small, the right somewhat the stronger. In fact really it is not a single portrait but a gallery of many generations. With an emphasis on the importance of being Suffolk.

I have just come across a description of one of these in a volume of newspaper cuttings—because our Victorian ancestors delighted in obituary notices, elegant funerals and all the trappings of mourning, hoarding them up for future delectation.

He was an old farmer at Culpho Hall, and, dying at 87 years of age and born at the beginning of the nineteenth century, his life spanned the whole era. He had lived in the same farmhouse all his life, from infancy to death, rocked in the cradle on that parlour chamber floor and dying in the bed in which he had been born. All his long life he had looked out of the windows on the same scene, the same pastures, the same revolving rotation of crops and labour. The old familiar round that had been known to all his fathers. Crowned by a harvest linked with other harvests down the years, the dates chalked up on the granary walls.

He was just old enough to remember the aftermath of the Napoleonic Wars, a glorious memory for farmers and landlords, but one of horror for the labourers. Then followed the collapse and depression until the Crimean War picked it up again and for twenty years agriculture never looked back. So his life was lived through prosperity and adversity until the end came, and all his farming goods and chattels were spread out in the field before the old house for yet another dispersal. And, be it noted, a Ransome's plough headed the list.

Reminiscences of the past crowded into the memory at those

Suffolk.

Santon Downham.

Lakenheath.

Eriswell

Mildenhall

Euston.

Banningham. Hinde

Honington. Botesdale

Freckenham Icklingham Hepworth

Ot. Livermere Ixworth Gislingham

Wordwell Ampton Gt. Livermere

Herringswell Badwell

Fornham St. Geneveve. Pakenham.

Kentford Risby Fornham St. Martin Norton.

NEWMARKET Gazeley Barrow Lt. Saxham BURY Elmswell

Moulton ST. EDMUNDS Haughley

Denham Hessett Woolpit

Chevington Ot. Welnetham Rattlesden.

Lidgate STOWMARKET

Hawstead Bradfield Combust. Combs

Stanningfield Bodley

Wickham brook Cockfield NEEDHAM MAR

Denston. Ringshall

Stradishall Hawkedon Hitcham Preston

Stansfield Bildeston.

Boxted LAVENHAM Nedging

Kedington Cavendish Long Melford Monks Eleigh Whatfi

HAVERHILL Clare Acton Lindsey Groton

SUDBURY Newton Boxford

Assington Lt. W

Polstead

Higham

NAYLAND

Wissington. Stratford St. Mary.

N.

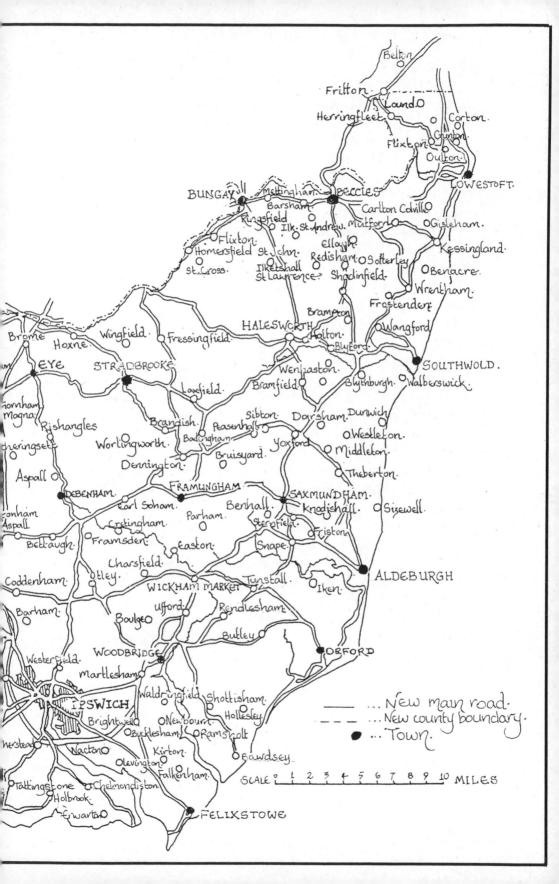

Belton

Fritton
Lound O
Herringfleet
Flixton
Oulton
Corton
Gunton

LOWESTOFT

BUNGAY
Mettingham
BECCLES
Carlton Colville
Barsham
Ringsfield
Ilk. St. Andrew.
Mutford
Gisleham.
Flixton
Ellough.
Kessingland.
Homersfield
St. John.
Redisham
Sotterley
St. Cross.
Ilketshall
St. Lawrence.
Shadinfield.
Benacre.
Wrentham.
Frostenden

Brampton
Wangford
Wingfield
Fressingfield.
HALESWORTH
Holton.
Blyford.
SOUTHWOLD
Brome
Hoxne
EYE
STRADBROOKE
Wenhaston
Bramfield.
Blythburgh.
Walberswick.
Loxfield.
Thornham
Magna
Rishangles
Brandish.
Peasenhall.
Sibton
Darsham.
Dunwich.
Westleton.
Heringsett
Worlingworth.
Badingham.
Yoxford
Middleton.
Aspall O
Dennington.
Bruisyard.
Theberton.
onham
Aspall
DEBENHAM.
FRAMLINGHAM
SAXMUNDHAM.
Bettaugh.
Earl Soham.
Benhall.
Knodishall.
Sizewell.
Cretingham.
Parham.
Stemfield.
Framsden.
Easton.
Snape.
Friston.
Coddenham.
Charsfield.
Otley.
WICKHAM MARKET
Tunstall.
ALDEBURGH
Barham.
Ufford.
Iken.
Boulge O
Rendlesham.
Westerfield.
Butley.
WOODBRIDGE
ORFORD
Martlesham.
herstead
IPSWICH
Waldringfield
Shottisham.
Brightwell.
Hollesley.
Newbourn.
Wacton O
Bucklesham.
Ramsholt.
Kirton.
Olevington.
Falkenham.
Bawdsey.
Tattingstone
Chelmondiston.
Holbrook
Erwarton

SCALE 0 1 2 3 4 5 6 7 8 9 10 MILES

FELIXSTOWE

——— ... New main road.
– – – ... New county boundary.
● ... Town.

dispersals of dead men's goods. Things their hands had made smooth with years of labour, and which other hands would continue to use until they were spent.

Now follows a minor portrait of an old Suffolk labourer. His cottage home, unlike the farmer's, was built soon after the accession of the young Victoria, two rooms up and two rooms down. It stood on a long strip of land fenced off from an adjoining field and contained about an acre. He had planted fruit trees about his little home and they were all bearing well. He had pigsties and fowl houses, so he was above average for his position in the social scale. Close by the cottage was a well, 75 feet deep, which had something of a history.

It was sunk by an old soldier who had taken part in the famous charge of the Light Brigade and had survived to return to his Suffolk village. It appears that in well-sinking the brickwork lining was suspended in it by iron rods from the top. As the well was dug the brickwork was allowed gradually to descend and was correspondingly added to with fresh courses at the top.

The old soldier had got near 70 feet down when the suspending rods snapped and went down like spears. Those at the top feared the worst, instead of which a voice came from the depths calling to be hauled up. The rods had fallen round him but he was un-scathed. A second time his life had been spared.

The account returns to the old labourer. The writer knocked on the door, which was opened by the housekeeper, for the old man's wife had been dead many a year. The caller was greeted with the familiar old country custom, "Would you like to see him?" "Yes, I should if you please," came the answer. So she led the way upstairs, into the quiet little bedroom, and on the bed was the white sheet raised in the middle by the body of the dead countryman. Pathetic, yet not morbid; he had returned to his fathers and would soon be mingled with their dust.

These two little portraits, miniatures would be more correct, are of peaceful times. Rejoicing in the fact that life had been spent in one place, the home of their fathers. Yet one of them had travelled far, perchance through agricultural depression, and had been thrust into an historic event which is being written about and discussed to this very day. A story of faultless but fruitless courage.

Two world wars separate us from those placid years, and we pick up our papers to read—the world is changing and we have to change with it. One is inclined to retort, have we not already changed? Is not the pace so rapid that those in years find themselves born in one era and overtaken by another? And there is a fear latent in many hearts, that the old forebodings may become a reality. In fact

> The world is too much with us; late and soon,
> Getting and spending, we lay waste our powers;

One thing can be truly said about our fathers, they were always looking forward. Even the old men would announce, as evening grew on, they were getting ready for the morning. So be it.

> The rainbow comes and goes,
> And lovely is the rose,
> The moon doth with delight
> Look round her when the heavens are bare,
> Waters on a starry night
> Are beautiful and fair:
> The sunshine is a glorious birth:
> But yet I know, where'er I go,
> That there hath passed away a glory from the earth.

Suffolk has been fortunate in its distinguished roll of county families. This evokes such names as the Herveys of Ickworth, the Graftons of Euston Hall, the Cadogans of Culford, the Stradbrokes of Henham. Followed by the Barnardistons and the Tollemaches, probably the oldest families of them all. Of the latter it is said, the name is thought to be a corruption of the term 'tollmock', tolling the bell. When the baronetcy was established in 1611, a Tollemache was one of the first to be so dignified.

Then come the Gooch family of Benacre, the Sir Joshua Rowleys and the Cobbolds. The point is that nearly all these names still appear in the lists of those who have the welfare of the county at heart and who are willing to lead the way.

Lord Gwydyr of Stoke Park, Ipswich, was one of the most interesting of the old guard. He was born in 1810 and lived to be within a day or two of his centenary, dying in 1910. He succeeded his cousin, the twenty-second Lord Willoughby de Eresby, in

1870. He saw the rise and fall of thirty governments, lived through five reigns and was present at three coronations. At his death he was the oldest peer in the House of Lords. Moreover, he had been an intimate friend of Napoleon III and the Empress Eugenie.

Another interesting personality was Colonel George Tomline of Orwell Park, Nacton. When he died it was said of him: "Another of the great figures of our local life has passed away and, in some respects the most remarkable of them all. Great in his talents, great in his wealth, great in his enterprises . . . the ruler over the destinies of so many scores of desirable farms, the lord of an army of gamekeepers and dependants, the king in fact of a little principality. . . . He seemed to have real love of opposition and fighting. In fact he gave the impression of being a spoilt child."

Directly the Education Act was passed he closed the school which he had supported. It was the same with the Agricultural Holdings Act, which contained clauses guaranteeing compensation to tenants for improvements. When a deputation of his tenants waited on him about a reduction of rent, he answered by ejecting some from their farms.

He had no family ties and paid no regard to public opinion. On one occasion he went with a lady friend to hear Spurgeon preach, and was introduced to the great preacher in his vestry. Spurgeon was sitting drinking sherry and asked his visitor to join him.

When he died in 1889, the disposal of his body was kept a strict secret, but it turned out he wished to be cremated, a rather rare and debatable process. He was only the ninety-third to be so dealt with at Woking, then the only crematorium in England. The body was taken from No. 1 Carlton House Terrace to St. Martin-in-the-Fields and thence to Waterloo Station. The account of the funeral also gave a detailed description of the method of cremation, then so new. (The first official cremation took place in 1885—a Mrs. Pickersgill of Woking, well known in literary and scientific circles.)

But then Suffolk had some women who distinguished themselves, notably Mary Beale, born at Barrow, near Bury. Her father, the Reverend John Cradock, was the rector, and baptised her 2nd March 1633. She married Charles Beale on 8th March 1651. He was a member of the Officers of Green Cloth, an amateur painter and a maker of artists' colours. He was lord of the manor of Walton on Thames.

Mary has been described as one of the best female painters of the seventeenth century, and she was employed by many of the most distinguished persons of her time. She painted in oils and water-colours, besides working in crayon. Her heads are very often surrounded by an oval border, painted in imitation of carved stone. Her pictures have often been attributed to Lely and Kneller; it was said the former was in love with her. She commenced her career in Suffolk, probably at Bury, and some of her work was at Hengrave Hall.

It is surely good to think that Suffolk also produced a number of writers for children, even if they have been called a 'monstrous regiment'. First comes Anne Laetitia Barbauld (1743–1825). She acquired learning at an early age, so she was evidently something of a prodigy, and published poems in 1773 and with her brother some prose essays. She married the Reverend Rochemont Barbauld in 1774 and established a boys' school at Palgrave, where her *Hymns in Prose for Children* were written. The school was given up in 1785, when she published a selection of English prose and poetry, presumably *Evenings at Home* in six volumes. She also produced *The Female Speaker* and a poem entitled *Eighteen Hundred and Eleven*, a verse of which Macaulay put into the mouth of his 'New Zealander'.

Her verse was of considerable merit, as this one on 'The Death of the Virtuous':

> So fades a summer cloud away;
>   So sinks the gale when storms are o'er;
> So gently shuts the eye of day;
>   So dies a wave along the shore.

But I wonder how many who seek out churchyard inscriptions, realize that she wrote:

> Say not "Good-night;" but in some brighter clime
>   Bid me "Good-morning."

One of her contemporaries was Mrs. Trimmer, born Sarah Kirby at Framlingham in 1741. She was the granddaughter of John Kirby, author of the famous *Suffolk Traveller*. She married

James Trimmer in 1762 and had twelve children. Whatever may
be said about her stern religious outlook she was a pioneer in the
education of small children by the use of pictures. She was
fascinated by Watt's little book of *Divine Songs Attempted in Easy
Language for the Use of Children*, and commended them to her
Sunday-school readers as the most delightful work ever written
for children. In 1789 she published *A Comment on Dr. Watt's
Divine Songs*. Her *Fabulous Histories* was produced by Longman
in 1786, the title of which was changed to the *History of the Robins*.
In 1802 she founded a periodical called *The Guardian of Education*,
wherein she made a notorious attack on fairy tales.

Six volumes of *Sacred History* were produced 1782–4. These
contained a series of prints with explanation. She also covered
English and Roman history. Each series consisted of engravings
to be displayed on the nursery or schoolroom walls. In 1824 she
reconstructed Sarah Fielding's (the sister of Henry) *The Governess*,
omitting what she regarded as undesirable, especially the fairy
tales, although she retained one.

Now follow Ann Taylor (1782–1866) and Jane (1783–1827).
They lived with their father and brother, both Isaacs, in Shilling
Old Grange, Shilling Street, Lavenham. The house with its three
gables in the roof is still there. We cannot claim them entirely for
Suffolk because they moved into Essex, but I like to think that
Jane looked out to the night sky through those old leaded
windows when she wrote:

> Twinkle, twinkle, little star,
> How I wonder what you are!

Both sisters came under the influence of Watts and published
Hymns for Infants' Minds in 1808, but they may have moved into
the sister county by then. However, if we claim the 'Star' for
Suffolk, perhaps we may also claim 'The Field Daisy', written
by Ann—at least I hope so.

> I'm a pretty little thing,
> Always coming with the spring;
> In the meadows green I'm found,
> Peeping just above the ground.
> And my stalk is covered flat,
> With a white and yellow hat.

Little lady, when you pass
Lightly o'er the tender grass,
Skip about, but do not tread
On my meek and healthy head,
For I always seem to say,
"Surely winter's gone away."

It was also Ann who wrote:

Who ran to help me when I fell,
And would some pretty story tell,
Or kiss the place to make it well?
My Mother.

Neither should we forget that Agnes Strickland, who wrote *The Queens of England*, also wrote for children: *The Moss House* and *The Rival Crusoes*.

But it was a Suffolk painter who created a lady's hat, known as the Gainsborough, with one side turned up.

It must not be forgotten too that the county has to record with pride that it produced one of the great regiments of the British Regular Army, now unfortunately no more. This was the old Twelfth, otherwise known as the "Swedebashers", with a regimental march "Speed the Plough", and a motto *Stabilis* or "Steady".

Its first colonel appropriately enough was Henry Howard, one of the great names of Suffolk history through Framlingham. It has been said that until 1914 their last known historical battle fought in Europe was at Minden in 1759, when the British infantry moving forward to the attack plucked roses to wear in their caps as they moved into position at early dawn. This tradition has always been observed on 1st August. It was so in the Great War of 1914–18.

But the fact is that the regiment was in most events. It was at the storming of Seringapatam, where it captured eight out of the eleven colours of Sultan Tippoo, six of which are at the Royal Hospital at Chelsea. Curiously enough they missed that famous Battle of Waterloo, as also the Peninsular War, the Crimea and the Indian Mutiny.

But they had a great history before that, when their story as a

Suffolk regiment began in 1742. It was then that an ensign carried the Colours at a parade at Blackheath whose name was James Wolf, later to become the hero of Quebec. They were at Dettingen when the last English king led his troops, which entitled them to wear a rose on his birthday. They were also a part of the garrison of the great siege of Gibraltar 1779–82, which provided them later on with a badge of a castle and key.

In 1881 the old Twelfth became the Suffolk Regiment, but it had marched with Lord Roberts to Kabul in 1878, an association that was to be repeated in 1900 when the 1st Battalion entered Pretoria with him. It had taken part in the Colesburg disaster before that.

The Great War of 1914–18, in which they were to lose nearly 7,000 officers and men, saw them in it at the start, taking part in such great events as the Battle of Le Cateau, Neuve Chapelle, Ypres and Loos. It was at the last mentioned that the regiment gained its first V.C., won by Sergeant A. F. Saunders of the 9th Battalion. One of their casualties was Captain Charles Sorley of D Company, who was described by Robert Graves as one of the three poets of importance to be killed in that war. They were at Mudros in 1916.

When the 11th Battalion arrived in France in 1916 an officer wrote: "The men are as happy as sandboys. They spend a great deal of time in inspecting and passing judgement on cattle, poultry and the like, one stalwart got up two hours before reveille today to admire the way French women milked." From which it was evident that the old way of home life was still uppermost in their thoughts. The second V.C. was won at Hagicourt by Corporal Sidney Day.

This year also saw the 1st Battalion in Palestine, with Gaza as one of their scenes of action.

Six battalions took part in the Battle of the Somme, when such names as La Boiselle, Albert, Pozieres, Delville Wood and Thiepval had significant and bloody memories. Later came Arras and that awful record of Passchendaele.

In 1935 the regiment celebrated the two hundred and fiftieth anniversary of its formation. The commemoration began with a dinner of the South African Veterans in the Town Hall, Bury St. Edmunds. This was attended by nearly a hundred. The regimental chapel in St. Mary's was dedicated by the bishop on Sunday, 25th June.

In 1939 came the Second War and the 1st Battalion in France in October, so soon to be evacuated via Dunkirk, and then posting off to Singapore. In May 1940 the 7th Battalion was reformed, to become known as "The String and Cardboard Suffolks". However, its life was short for it became the 142nd Regiment of the Royal Armoured Corps, which was disbanded in 1944. Then in 1956 the 1st were in Cyprus.

But the last great conflict brought about a change in warfare, as it was to see the end of such a proud regiment. Therefore on 1st September 1964 the old Twelfth became part of the 1st Royal Anglian Regiment, and its identity was gone.

It suffices to say that when the Colours were laid up in the regimental chapel, they bore not only the Castle and Key of Gibraltar, but such names as Dettingen, Minden, Seringapatam and India. Neither should we forget that some of the regiment were in the ill-fated *Birkenhead* and that a tablet to their memory is in St. Mary's.

Configuration and Early Settlers

Since time whereof no memory is.

Suffolk has been always a fair county, its fortunes founded on good earth. That Suffolk was once, possibly more than once, submerged by the sea is evidenced by its various stratified beds, particularly so in its coralline crag deposits. It rests solidly on the famous London Clay, so named because it forms the foundation of London itself and extends into Hampshire and the Isle of Wight. This provided the brick earth when Suffolk brick kells (kilns) figured so largely as local industries, as also in the local stone known as septaria, dredged up from the sea.

A geologists' paradise was created at Bramford, near Ipswich, where a great pit was laid bare as in a panorama. Working upwards, white chalk to 60 feet; lower eocene beds to 15 feet; detritus bed, where flint implements were found, to 3 feet; decalcified red crag to 15 feet; middle glacial gravel to 15 feet; contorted clayey ground to 5 feet.

It is evident that early man existed in these parts from the scrapers and implements found in these beds. For example, a most beautiful reaping hook was unearthed at Felixstowe, when one of its most historic fields was recently being bulldozed for a housing estate near the coast. These ancient men knew the art of flaking to an eminent degree.

It is interesting to note, in these days of packaged holidays, that during the Eocene period we had a climate equalled only today by the Philippine Islands, with fauna and flora to match.

Dr. J. E. Taylor, lecturing in 1891, made this very interesting point, speaking of the alluvial soil:

In this thin veneer of living vegetable soil you see at the top, which men have turned over for ages past, from which we extract our

Hadleigh Vale, a rolling patchwork of fields established by the early settlers

daily bread by agricultural operations, which may sometimes, according to the nature of the subsoil, go down two or three feet, or keep within the space of nine or ten inches—in this veneer there are locked up all the material vestiges of the people who formerly inhabited this county. The Romans, the Ancient Britons whom they subdued and dominated, the Saxons and Danes with their fiercely contested tribal fights—all these left traces of an occupation extending over many hundreds of years, and yet the whole archaeological record is contained within a few inches of soil.

In his *Geology of Suffolk*, published in 1884, Dr. Taylor describes the various strata as follows.

The Chalk. This has an extensive geographical distribution extending continuously from Norfolk, under Bury St. Edmunds, in the western division of the county, to Ipswich on the southeast. Towards the southern parts of Suffolk the chalk is lost sight of, and is overlaid by Eocene strata, which here reach their northern extension.

The London Clay is well developed in the southern parts of Suffolk, and especially in the triangular area between the rivers Orwell and Stour. The London Clay may be said to constitute the substratum of all districts intensified by the estuaries of the south-east of Suffolk, and the coast section from Orford Ness to Walton-on-the-Naze, in Essex. The London Clay is a rich, bluish-black, marine mud. Its blue colour is due to the presence of carbonate of iron. In some cases it is crowded with organic remains. This provided the septaria, the only local stone used in building our churches and walls. Very frequently, beautiful crystals of sulphate of lime, or selenite, were found in it. These were known as 'congealed water' by quarrymen. This clay was dug up to provide the Roman cement and produced the best wheat.

The Suffolk Bone Bed produced the box stones underlying the Coralline and Red Crag beds. The area where these are most abundant ranges from Foxhall near Ipswich to Felixstowe. Box stones are rolled nodules of hard brown sandstone of which 20 per cent contain remains of shells.

The Coralline Crag is a calcareous sand deposit full of fossil shells. In some cases it was so hard that it was quarried for building stone. Its chief deposit was in the neighbourhood of Sudbourne.

The Red Crag, which as well as the Coralline Crag, is chiefly limited to Suffolk and the adjoining parts of Essex.

Chillesford Clay was a bed of fine clay to be found in that area. At that place was unearthed almost the entire skeleton of a whale. The clay was nearly as thick at Aldeburgh and was used for brick making. Norwich Crag was to be found at Thorpeness and Bulcamp.

About the middle of last century at Kessingland, a man named Davis, more familiarly known as 'Robinson Crusoe', lived in a hut of his own construction. He was quite independent of the female sex, his sole companion being a cat. He maintained himself by cultivating a small piece of ground, and also by collecting and selling bones which he found along the coast. His hut was a small museum of curiosities. Archaeologists wondered what they had lost by his activities.

Suffolk is not flat as so many casual observers would have us believe, but has many pleasant undulations which present a smiling countryside. It has also the peculiarity of the Brecklands in the north-west and the Sandlings along the coast. These were caused by the chalk surface, for many years subject to strong winds, producing a land of little growth. These have been scientifically afforested and made productive. The Sandlings made splendid sheep walks and provided an excellent soil for carrots.

Sir John Sinclair, in his valuable work *The Code of Agriculture*, has this: "The carrot husbandry in the Sandlings of Suffolk, as they are called, is one of the most interesting objects to be met with in British agriculture. After all expenses are defrayed, the profit is considerable, and the carrots are found to be an admirable preparation for other crops. Some prefer fattening bullocks with them; while others, who have the advantage of water carriage, think it most beneficial to send them to London market."

An article in the *Victoria County History* asserts that the county of Suffolk offers the nearest approach to an epitome of the Stone Age of man that is probably to be found in the whole world.

In a line drawn from Thetford to Bury St. Edmunds, thence to Mildenhall, Lakenheath, Brandon and back to Thetford are some of the richest deposits of the Palaeolithic Age in England, if not in the world.

Neolithic implements all lie on or in the surface soil. A valley that runs from the plateau of Elveden to the main valley of the Lark is from the Neolithic point of view probably one of the richest deposits in the world. It consists of only some 300 acres, but here are many thousands of such implements.

The variety of the Neolithic implements found in Suffolk is very great and the beauty of them is not to be surpassed in the British Isles. An interesting suggestion has been put forward that long chipped axes had their main uses in hollowing out of canoes. These were made from tree trunks, along the underside of which as they lay on the ground, fires were lit and the charred wood was then stubbed out by these flint implements. Scrapers have been found in larger numbers in Suffolk than anywhere else. Arrow heads also, of the three types: leaf-shaped, lozenge-shaped and the barbed and tanged variety. Then come javelin heads, spear heads, knife daggers, chisels, axe hammers and hammer heads.

The Bronze Age ushered in a new race of people and marked a great change in burial customs. Cremation was then first started; but, of course, inhumation continued.

Hoards of bronze antiquities comprise a considerable variety of new and old implements, ingots of rough metal or cakes of copper. These fall into three groups—personal hoards, merchants' hoards, founders' hoards—and they have been found at Clare, Felixstowe, Thornham and Exning. Unearthed recently on the Aldeburgh golf course was a Bronze Age urn that might well date back to about 1,400 B.C.

A gold torc was found at Boyton, and five others at Belstead, with another nearby, making six in all from the Ipswich area. It seems remarkable when one reads that they are one of the most important archaeological finds ever made in this country. The most beautiful specimen of these personal ornaments was made at Snettisham: it is now described as the Snettisham Torc and has given its name to the style of the decoration.

The Ipswich specimens are outstanding examples of early Celtic craftsmanship, made of gold mixed with silver, but, unlike the Snettisham example, they are unfinished. This condition reveals the method of manufacture: the twisted gold threads are inserted into large hollow terminals. They were discovered on 26th October 1968, during mechanical earth-moving operations, declared treasure trove and the British Museum exercised its option and acquired them. An *ex gratia* payment of £45,000 was paid, the highest price then paid by the British Museum for treasure trove. One has plain ring terminals, while the others are beautifully decorated in the Snettisham style. The fifth torc was found in 1970.

The Early Iron Age succeeded the Bronze and ended with the coming of the Romans. The iron may have been imported by the Brythons, a branch like the Goidels or Bronze Age people of the Celtic family.

An Early Iron Age burial deposit of great interest was discovered about 1888 at Elveden. This was examined by Arthur Evans (later Sir Arthur, the discoverer of Knossos). He drew attention to the fact that it was almost exactly like such a find at Aylesford, Kent. A tankard of this period was also ploughed up here. A brooch was found on a skeleton at Lakenheath and a very interesting group was found when draining Millpost Field at Westhall in 1855.

As far as palaeontology is concerned, the claim of Suffolk to a foremost position among English counties is based on the mammalian and other fossils found in the Red and Coralline Crags. These include such creatures as the cave-lion, otter, grizzly bear, wolf, red deer, bison, mammoth, wild horse, rhinoceros, hyena, elephant, mastodon, opossum and monkey. Then there are remains of various kinds of whales, porpoises and dolphins. Sharks have also been found, turtles and even an albatross.

The chief industries connected with geology are lime-burning and brick making. Woolpit brick has been famous since the time of Queen Elizabeth I. When Sir Morton Peto made the esplanade at Lowestoft, he protected the cliff at Kirkley by tipping a lot of boulder clay down the face of the cliff. It was a bed of fine loam that produced the Lowestoft China, 1756–1802. London Clay when exposed becomes a rich loam. Only in the neighbourhood of Newmarket does the chalk present the characteristic feature of open downs with short, springing turf.

Suffolk possesses no remarkable mineral water. Chalybeate springs have been observed here and there, but none has attained any fame. In fact the only noteworthy wells are those dedicated to saints. The main features over a great part of England were

sculptured prior to the Glacial period, but the main features of
Suffolk are of a subsequent date.

Evidence of the antiquity of man was obtained at a very early
date in Suffolk, although its significance was not realized until
long after. Thus, in the year 1797, John Frere called attention to
the finding of stone implements at Hoxne.

Breckland was one of the most thickly populated districts of
England in those prehistoric days, and is crossed by three ancient
trackways: the Icknield Way, also known as Icknield Street,
Peddars Way, and the Drove. W. G. Clarke writes:

> At one period there was a ridge of the oldest soil, Kimmeridge
> clay, or lower greensand, gault and chalk, stretching between
> Swaffham and Newmarket. The great eastern glacier crossing from
> north-west to south-east across the present fen basin, from which
> it removed most of the Kimmeridge clay, would cut away most of
> the chalk ridge and carry the detritus of the two foundations to the
> south-eastern extension of its *moraine profonde*, as evidenced by the
> chalky boulder clay which overspreads so much of Suffolk. After
> chalk and gault had been in great part removed, the glacier would
> cut into the greensand but would not push the detritus so far as this,
> and this I take to be the very sand, with plenty of chalk, though
> usually in small pieces, and is so different in appearance from our
> ordinary clay, as hardly to be recognized as such. . . . With a loose
> soil in a comparatively treeless country there would be a tendency
> to further decalcification of the chalky boulder clay, and its dis-
> tribution would also be affected by the wind, much of the present
> depths of sand in some areas having been undoubtedly blown there.

Clarke, who gave the Brecklands their name, goes on to say:

> The tracks from south-west, generally known as the Icknield Way,
> pass through Royston and Newmarket, cross the Kennett at
> Kentford and enter Breckland at Cavenham, between which and
> Lackford Bridge the track is over Cavenham heath.
>   Though there is little doubt that the Icknield Way crossed the
> river Lark at what is now Lackford Bridge, and thence followed
> the boundary of the Blackbourne at Lackford Hundred to Thetford,
> some confusion has been caused by two ancient ways, which crossed
> the river further westward, one at Temple Bridge, west of
> Icklingham St. James, and the other a little west of the Pilgrims'
> Path, which runs north-east from Icklingham All Saints Church.

This is what Henry Prigg (who later changed his name to Trigg) had to say about it in his *Icklingham Papers*:

There is probably no part of the kingdom, for its extent, more prolific in antiquities than the North West district of Suffolk. From its soil have been recovered relics of the earliest men with whom we are at present acquainted, who certainly dwelt there in considerable numbers, and who shared the county with a variety of animals which have ceased to exist here, and some of whom have become totally extinct. These men after a lapse of unknown ages were succeeded by the men of the later stone age and the fierce Celt, both of whom have left us traces of their lengthy sojourn in the district, in the numerous weapons of stone and heaped-up mounds under which repose the ashes of their chieftains. In no part of England save in the Yorkshire Wolds, or the plains around the vast megalithic monuments of Stonehenge, are tumuli more numerous than here. The open country, the dryness of the soil, the contiguity of the woods and marshes of the fens, with game of all kinds in abundance, rendered the locality an attractive one to all the earlier people, whose encampments, during the pastoral stage of their existence, doubtless dotted the plains and brooksides at no very distant intervals. As time went on and the cultivation of the soil became a necessity men settled down in communities and so originated our villages and from them our towns. Between these communication was required and so the great trackways grew into existence and the British oppidum which then occupied portions of what is now the parish of Icklingham All Saints, came to be united with the neighbouring settlements towards the interior of the county, by what was known as the Icknield-way, or as the late Dr. Guest suggests the Icknield weg, the war or battle road of the Iceni.

The Peddars Way is described thus by W. G. Clarke: "... another prehistoric track, adapted and improved by the Romans. It crosses Norfolk in a south-easterly direction from the coast-line at Holme to Blackwater, a ford on the Little Ouse some four miles east of Thetford, and thence into Suffolk. Although its continuity is now somewhat broken, in its original condition it was the largest and straightest local road, and the one that most avoided known habitations."

Again: "The Drove Road is neither so long nor so important a prehistoric trackway as the previous two, but is entirely within the confines of Breckland, and is in some respects more interesting than either of the two more famous roads."

And this is what Edward Thomas said in his book about the Icknield Way: "There were a number of things I should have seen near Lackford, such as the burial mound north of Culford church, wittily called the 'Hill of Health', and the road between Pakenham and Stowlangtoft called Bull Road, and some of the moats, at Maulkin's Hall and other 'Halls' of Suffolk. But the Icknield Way turned sharp to the right out of the road I had taken, opposite Lower Farm, soon after the ford of the Lark. When it was more important than the eastward road to Bury the Way curved round westward beyond the river, and its old course is marked by a depression through the furze on the right which finally reaches the present road and is lost in it."

Another ancient earthwork is the Devil's Dyke at Newmarket, where it is alleged dwelt the Iceni, who, according to R. C. Lyle in his *Royal Newmarket,*

were famous for their horsemanship, their scythed chariots, and their revolt against the Romans under Boadicea. After defeat they were permitted to retain their kingdom with its metropolis at the rude barbaric settlement at Exning, under a system of vassalage and tribute to Rome. Their gold and silver coinage, possibly stamped for the purpose of paying tribute, bore on the reverse side the effigy of a horse.

The Devil's Dyke, that great landmark, was associated with horses and warlike scenes. This formidable mount, dominating the Heath, strikes northwards across its expanse in a straight course of eight miles. Its right flank rests upon streams and fenland, and its left upon forest land. In all probability it was intended to guard against invasion from the West, and as a consequence, it slopes steeply on the eastern side, measuring about ninety feet from the summit of the escarpment to the bottom of the Ditch excavated at its foot.

Probably the lofty rampart thus reared against the tide of invading hordes was further rendered impregnable by stakes and palisades. But the most interesting feature of the Devil's Dyke is the eighteen-foot way, or causus, along its top, sufficiently wide for the passage of chariots or cavalry. Fragments of bronze chariot wheels have been discovered in recent years.

Who constructed the Devil's Dyke? Some say the Iceni, to protect their strategically weak boundaries. Other ascribe it to the Roman legions in occupation of the country. Others unworthily hold it to be of no defence work at all, but some kind of drainage scheme for the fens. This dull suggestion need not concern us, considering the skeleton of a warrior and the flint arrow heads discovered in the course of excavations.

During the Norman period, the Dyke became known as St. Edmund's Dyke, because the jurisdiction of the abbots of Bury St. Edmunds extended westwards this far. But this did not last long.

When, at an early date, Exning, the Iceni settlement, was stricken by a plague, its market was removed to the adjoining village, where a new market was set up. Thus Newmarket received its name.

Naturally enough there is plenty of folk-lore in these districts. A small rapid stream runs through the village of Exning, in which were pickerel (young pike). It was said that in the severest winters the part passing the vicarage was never frozen.

It would appear that before the Iceni (Spurden the philologist speaks of Icenian counties and Icenisms), Suffolk was populated by Early Britons. That these were nothing to run after as progenitors of our race is brought out in the apocryphal story as told by St. Guthlac of Croydon (Crowland) to prove their existence in Fenlands at a period long posterior to their conquest by the Angles. The saint, being disturbed one night by horrid howling, was seriously alarmed, thinking that the howlers might be Britons. Upon looking out he discovered that they were only devils, whereby he was comforted, the Britons being the worse of the two.

When the Romans came they were welcomed by the settlers who saw in them a protective force, and they all settled down to live together. This went on until the Romans became rather aggressive, and although the Iceni fought well and truly against them, they had not much chance.

The Romans brought their own culture with them, and built their own type of houses and roads. Their troops manned the vantage points that would keep the conquered island safe from intruders. The officers kept apart from the native Britons, but many soldiers married native wives and their children settled down as local farmers. Much pottery was imported, but later kilns developed in Britain: there was one at Long Melford. Metal artifacts were also made in Suffolk: a workshop site has been excavated at Hacheston. When Roman generals departed

in A.D.407, taking the last of the much depleted army, Suffolk had already been agriculturally self-sufficient for many generations.

The Romans came here in the middle of the first century A.D., and left in the fifth century. It would appear that on the eve of their invasion the greater part of Suffolk was left uninhabited by the Iceni, who were living in the open country to the west. It is well known that upon the capitulation of the Trinobantes the Iceni came to terms with Rome and were given a partial and patronized freedom, but it did not last long. There was a definite Roman penetration in the south-east and south-west of our county. The revolt by Boudicca has nothing to do with Suffolk. Traces of the Roman period are dotted about all over the county. They can be grouped under two heads, military and civil, of which the first is the more important.

Colchester was the great centre of Roman activity in East Anglia, which may account for the paucity of remains in Ipswich of their occupation. Moreover, it was south Suffolk that chiefly felt the first impact of the invasion. The chief Roman road ran from Colchester to Caistor-by-Norwich, identified as Iter IX in the Antonine Itineraries—the Roman road book—and known to antiquaries as the Pye road. It entered Suffolk at Stratford St. Mary, continuing via Capel St. Mary, to cross the Gipping at Baylham Mill, and thence to Scole along the main Ipswich–Norwich road. A branch leaves this road north of Coddenham and goes via Pettaugh and Earl Soham to Peasenhall. Nothing is known of it beyond this point apart from a track across the heath to Dunwich. At Stratford St. Mary, the road is presumed to have crossed the Stour by an old pile bridge.

Another road appears to have entered the county at Bungay, parallel with the Weybread–Peasenhall Road, and then to follow the line of Stone Street to Halesworth, and possibly over the Blyth at Blyford, where a statuette of Venus was found; and so to Dunwich.

There appears to have been a Route V between Colchester and Lincoln to Carlisle, but it has no satisfactory course through Suffolk. It is thought, however, that Villa Faustini and Icinos must have been somewhere in the county.

The stream at Exning, a subject of early folk-lore

A Roman way also crossed the county in a south-easterly direction from Thetford to Ixworth, Woolpit and Bildeston to Stratford St. Mary; and the names of Norton Street, Fen Street and Low Street indicate the route. A road is also conjectured to have extended from the Waveney, near Lopham Ford, through Ixworth to Bury. On this line appears the two villages of Stanton and a place called Up-street Lane.

Suckling remarks: "These numerous roads, which thus spread over Suffolk like so many arteries in the system of Roman subjugation, terminated at strong fortresses, and afforded expeditious means of communication with the intermediate stations."

The Saxon Shore fort at Burgh Castle was built in the late third century, and the occupation seems to have reached its peak during the reign of Constantine I. It was occupied continuously down to the time of Honorius and the beginning of the fifth century. When Anglo-Saxon settlements reached sufficient importance in the seventh century, St. Fursey selected it as his missionary headquarters. After the Norman Conquest a castle of the motte and bailey type was probably built in the south-west corner of the fort, the fort wall being used as a bailey.

The fort is 640 feet long, by 413 feet wide. The walls are 9 feet thick, with foundations of 12 feet thick. It has three gateways and the remains of the west wall was unearthed in 1859 by Henry Harrod. These forts were capable of holding from 500 to 1,000 men. Breydon water may have been an anchorage for the fleet. Each of these stations had its own burial yard. Roman urns containing cremated remains were found here; they were made of a coarse blue clay, brought from Bradwell.

These stations ran from Pevensey in Sussex to Brancaster on the Wash, and the coast line received the name of *Litus Saxonicum*. Walton (Felixstowe) was another of these stations, and the mouth of the Deben may have acted as a harbour for the fleet.

Roman wells have been uncovered along the coast, one being at Covehithe. They were square in construction, timber framed, made of boards standing in sections one on top of another, and strengthened at the angles by cross-pieces. When they became dry they were used as rubbish dumps.

Dunwich, situated as it is about midway along the Suffolk coast, was probably another of these stations. It must have been at the end of a spur road, probably by way of Coddenham and Peasenhall, or by Burgh near Woodbridge and Stratford St. Andrew. In any case the road would have entered Dunwich at the Sandy Lane.

There is a path from a point known once upon a time as the 'Red Stile' at Westleton which leads straight across fields and joins the Darsham road, with the long straight road to Dunwich. In the opposite direction (westwards) a road runs for miles almost in a straight line to Heveningham, where it is called Dunwich Lane. This links up with Tonk's Lane, Cratfield, and has been described as an ancient British Way from Dunwich to Bury; and so on through Newmarket, Cambridge and St. Neots to the heart of the country.

Peddars Way is one of the most remarkable of the Roman roads on the east side of Britain, but does not appear in the Antonine Itineraries.

Roman sites occupied during the last decades of the first century and the first half of the second are at Barnham, Brandon, Capel St. Mary, Coddenham, Baylham Combs, Darmstead, Exning, Hazelwood, Hitcham, Holbrook, Ixworth, Kirton, Lakenheath, Long Melford, Reydon Smere, Wattisfield, Great Welnetham and West Stow.

Third- and fourth-century sites include Burgh Castle, Burgh near Woodbridge, Eye, Eriswell, Felixstowe and Icklingham, where considerable finds were made.

There were villas at Eye, Great Thurlow, Coddenham, West Row in Mildenhall, which places nearly cross the county. A Roman villa was excavated at Castle Hill, Whitton, Ipswich in 1933, and extensive finds were made including a mosaic pavement, the only one existing in Suffolk. There were also urns, bowls, rings, and what appear to have been apothecary's instruments. All these are now in the Ipswich Museum. Two bronze lions were dug up at Capel St. Mary, and a bronze boar at Wattisfield. A gold Roman bracelet was found near Burgh; and at Clopton in 1883 a boy found a gold Roman coin, which he sold to a watchmaker at Woodbridge.

Coin hoards have been found at Benacre and Lavenham. But one of the most remarkable of the coin hoards was found at Clent Farm near Eye in 1781. This consisted of several hundred gold coins enclosed in a leaden cist. At Stowlangtoft in a field about half a mile from the church, was found a pot full of Roman coins of the Lower Empire, in number about 12,400. This was in 1764. At Sutton a labourer digging for coprolites in 1870 came across a vessel said to have contained nearly a bushel of Roman coins.

A whole series of pewter plates was dug up at Icklingham, the remains of a great dinner service. A set of bronze bowls from another service was found at Santon Downham. All were British made, not imported. More probably imported was a statuette found at Barking Hall. It is considered to be of a Roman Emperor. The head of a great statue of Claudius, the emperor who planned the invasion in A.D. 43, was found in the River Alde.

One wonders how the Romans settled into our climate, certainly they built their houses in the way at home, with some sort of heating. How did they employ their spare time, and what sort of games did the children play? Did they bring them over from Rome, as they did 'stick and goose'? Or make them up when they got here?

When the Roman troops were withdrawn, possibly by Constantine III, the wealthier inhabitants deposited their savings and precious things and fled, never to return. The poorer classes had nothing to leave, but stayed behind to become assimilated amongst the newcomers.

One thing we are apt to gloss over is the gap of the years. Our next visitors were the Saxons, and until the discovery at Sutton Hoo they presented a very sketchy and incomplete picture. They also came with a high culture behind them, but were far more settlers than the Romans, so that an Anglo-Saxon race was formed. They even created a kingdom which was to include the North Folk, Cambridge and parts of Essex; and their work remains even to this day. They set boundaries and governors, parcelled out the land into manageable proportions. But it must be stressed there was something in these parts that they found worthy of their attention as a place in which to settle.

One might ask why it was that the bulge which sticks out into the North Sea was divided into two. The Waveney made a natural division between the South Folk and the North Folk. Moreover, there is a distinct difference between the two. When one crosses from Suffolk into Norfolk the flora is darker and there is no doubt as to which county one is in.

The language—that is the one before all the aids to its destruction had come into being, although it can be still detected—is much the same in both counties, with this difference. Whereas real Suffolkers speak with a kind of sing-song, Norfolk has a broader and more sustained note. The Saxon influence was very apparent in the children of the eastern half of the county, with their blue eyes and flaxen hair. But the people of the north-west of the county were much darker, almost celtic in appearance, with dark hair and dark eyes. When one considers the traditional character of Suffolk people and their slowness to welcome and weather 'furriners'—that is people from outside the county— in their midst, it is rather remarkable to realize that they stem from foreigners themselves. Certainly the Saxons were that, and invaders and alien conquerors to boot.

Many of the place-names are Anglo-Saxon, starting with Acton and ending with Yoxford, but those ending in *by*, such as Ashby and Barnby, are Danish.

Anglo-Saxon remains are dotted over most of the county, although it must be realized that most of their settlements were in the river valleys. A jewelled brooch was found at Sutton about 1835 by a ploughman; and a gold pendant at Palgrave in 1852. The most interesting object was the whalebone writing tablet, found at Blythburgh on the property of Mr. Seymour Lucas, R.A., who presented it to the British Museum in 1902. This is the only Anglo-Saxon specimen known.

A great many pieces of jewellery have been unearthed from burials, and they are thought to be local work, rather than done by immigrants. A large number of pieces were found at Ipswich. The swastica or fylfot as an ornamentation sometimes occurs. Signs of intercourse with Kent are very evident. Under an ancient oak on Wizard Farm at Wickham Skeith many Saxon coins of Harold and Edward the Confessor were found. These also are in the British Museum.

Suffolk's first known king was Redwald, who had broken away from dependence upon the Kentish kings. He built himself a palace at Rendlesham. He is supposed to have embraced Christianity, but in rather a tardy fashion, retaining his allegiance to heathenism. He was succeeded by a son, or more probably a nephew, Sigebert, who landed at Dunwich from exile in Burgundy. It was there he set up his kingdom and presumably built a palace. He was soon followed by a monkish friend named Felix, who set about Christianizing the locality. Sigebert had become a convert to Christianity in Gaul. Unfortunately tribal wars were the order of the day and the young king soon became a victim—not, however, before he had founded a monastery at Bury St. Edmunds, the Roman Beodricsworth. He was of the royal house of the Wuffingas. He went into battle carrying only a wand and was slain.

I cannot fail to see history repeating itself some 1,200 years later in the Great War. Lieutenant-Colonel C. H. M. Doughty-Wylie won a posthumous V.C. at Sedd-el-Bahr, Gallipoli. He was a Theberton man, not royal it is true but a great lover of the Turk, and went into action carrying only a cane.

The history of these Wuffingas was very obscure until the almost miraculous discovery of the ship burial at Sutton Hoo. As the treasures were uncovered and handled—as they could only have been handled at the present day—so their story seemed to unfold itself and become plain. It is not so much the priceless jewels, but the information they give of a high rate of culture, thus providing the missing pages of a great record. It is a breathtaking story, the more so when it is suggested that some of the jewellery is the work of local goldsmiths. Moreover, there seems to be a link with *Beowulf*, which was written down some hundred years after, and Sutton Hoo's burial might have provided matter for the description of the burial of Scyld Scefing.

> Then fell to earth the dark-hilted sword.
> No more would the earl hold the hard blade,
> Wielding his weapons. Yet still once more
> Spoke the grey warrior—urged his young men,
> Bade them go on, his loyal companions.
> He could not on foot any longer stand fast,
> But up to heaven looked:
> "Now do I thank Thee, Wielder of Nations,

For all the joys that in this world I had.
Merciful Master, now do I need Thee.
Grant Thou a boon upon my spirit,
That my soul may journey to Thee,
Into Thy kingdom, Lord of the angels,
Peaceful to pass."

The Battle of Maldon

To anyone who knew old Suffolk people of a generation or so ago, it would come as no surprise that the Sutton Hoo and the Mildenhall Treasures came to light. The old folks' memories and speech were deep in the past, and underground passages and hidden treasures were an everyday background.

A good example comes from the small village of Acton, which possesses that fine brass of Sir Roger de Bures, dated 1302. And where a century ago a small charity, known as Keddington's, supplied six widows with a small loaf each every Sunday and a pair of shoes yearly. One can be very sure that the widows were regular in their devotions at church.

A legend was current that on certain occasions, not specified, the park gates would fly open at midnight, *withouten hands*, and a carriage drawn by four spectral horses, accompanied by headless grooms and outriders would proceed swiftly from the park to a spot called the 'nursery corner'. This 'corner' tradition had it, was where a very bloody engagement took place when the Romans governed the county. However, few Roman remains have been found there.

Near this spot was Wimbell Pond, in which, according to local tradition, there was an iron chest full of money. If any person was daring enough to throw a stone into the water, it would ring against the chest. Whereupon a small white figure could be heard calling in a distressed voice, "That's mine!" (I must say I like the end bit.)

Battles long ago were well authenticated and every bit of rising ground had its story, although they got a bit mixed up as to dates. A few hundred years were glossed over as a tale that is told. But the fact remains that much of their old wives' tales have come true, a tribute to oral tradition.

The unearthing of the Sutton Hoo Ship-Burial, however, was an epoch-making event. The digging was begun by local archaeologists in 1939, but it was soon realized that it was of greater importance than they could handle. The mound had been rifled before but the thieves had not gone deep enough, and the burial chamber, like a deck house, had been left intact. This is what R. L. S. Bruce-Mitford has said about it: ". . . the Sutton Hoo grave is not just any ordinary chieftain's tomb, but a phenomenon of the first magnitude, even against the European background. It has implications in many fields."

The grave, or cenotaph, has been dated in the period A.D. 620–30 and three things found within it—helmet, shield and sword—together with such ceremonial items as the iron standard and the fascinating and enigmatic whetstone, surmounted by a ring with a splendid antlered stag on top. This has demonstrated beyond all dispute that the burial is of royal significance. Of the whetstone Dr. Bruce-Mitford quotes Dr. T. D. Kendrick as saying: "nothing like this monstrous stone exists anywhere else. It is a unique, savage thing; and inexplicable, except perhaps as a symbol, proper to the king himself, of the divinity and mystery which surrounds the smith and his tools in the northern world."

Sutton Hoo has been related to Rendlesham, where the old writers have asserted there was a royal palace, probably built by Redwald, an overlord. If a palace then a church, because this was the seat of the royal house of the Wuffingas. A crown of precious metal was dug up here about 1690, but was melted down before any particulars could be given to posperity. This is not the only evidence that links Rendlesham with the hypothetical palace. Field names recorded in 1840 speak of 'Hall Piece' and 'Hall Yard Piece'. The parish boundary has characteristics which belong to early estate boundaries where game was kept within the park limits. Anglo-Saxon kings loved hunting deer.

This spectacular find has led to all kinds of suppositions. If a royal burial, was it of an English king or a Swedish? Was he Christian or pagan? If English, then who was he? Where did the articles found within come from? What did they signify? To all of which questions it must be realized as Mr. Bruce-Mitford says: "It is an archaeological revelation without a direct documentary support." He also describes the finds as being among the outstanding treasures of the British Museum.

First, the Wuffingas have been listed, from Wehha, Wuffa, Tyttla to Redwald, who died 624 or 625, and on to Aelfwald, who died 740. Those who incline towards a Swedish king or dynasty, assert the whole affair to have been an importation, judging by certain of the contents, and the fact that ship burials were Swedish, and this an ocean-going boat.

Was he Christian? In many respects this appears to have been a pagan burial, by reason of the treasures accompanying the dead and the location of the tomb. But there remain the two silver spoons marked Saulus and Paulus, suggestive of a christening, and the set of silver bowls. It must be realized that Christianity was by this time well established in the kingdom, and if it was Christian the burial should have been in, or about, a church as this had then become the custom. The first Christian missionaries, of whom St. Felix at Dunwich was an example, concentrated on the royal courts. It was Siegebert who brought over the Burgundian missionary monk, when he ascended the throne and built him a church at Dunwich, according to Bede.

Who was he, if English? It might have been Redwald, who embraced Christianity and then reverted to paganism. A purse of coins, of which the latest is dated A.D. 618, rules out earlier opinions that it was Athelhere, killed at Winward, Yorkshire, in 655, or his brother Aethelwald, both sons of Ene, who did not himself reign. A Swede is also today discounted.

The next question concerns the treasures unearthed, their provenance and manufacture. Some have undoubtedly been proved Swedish, but others, particularly the cloisonne work, are English. If so, it suggests a high rate of culture in those early, almost unchartered years. Their significance lies in their prodigal wealth, suitable only for a great personage, either king or chieftain.

Further complications arise because of the complete absence of any trace of a body, buried or cremated. This makes it probable that it is a cenotaph to mark the spot of one lost in battle or drowned at sea.

Mr. Bruce-Mitford in his article "The Sutton Hoo Ship-Burial", published in the *Proceedings of the Suffolk Institute of Archaeology*, 1950, quotes Professor H. M. Chadwick as follows:

I find it impossible to believe that in the times with which we are concerned a treasure of such an amount and value can have belonged to anyone except a king. According to heroic standards then recognized all men of the highest rank were dependent on the king and expected to present to him, as their lord, everything that they acquired by their exploits—though doubtless they looked for rewards. We may refer to Beowulf, 2052 ff., where the hero on his return home, presents to the king and queen all the treasures which have been given to him at the Danish court. There is no evidence that England in the seventh century possessed a wealthy independent class, whether mercantile, industrial or professional.

It does not necessarily follow that the person buried or commemorated was himself a king. We know of extravagant funeral honours paid by kings to their mothers and wives; and this funeral may possibly have been in honour of the father or other near relation of a king. (If of Acthelhere, then it would have been Ene, who did not reign.) But on the whole it is not very likely. The great funerals we hear of in early Teutonic history and tradition are those of kings themselves. . . . After all events it is difficult to believe that a cenotaph on this scale can have been intended for anyone except a king.

However, the whole thing bristles with speculation, and the pious hope remains that some later discovery may elucidate the whole mystery. (Modern research suggests it was Redwald.)

The Mildenhall Treasure is something quite different, but its finding was no less spectacular. In this case it is undisputably Roman. It was found at West Row, Mildenhall, on the edge of the Fens, by two men who were ploughing. Their extraordinary discovery was held back for four years, being made known to the public in 1946 by a doctor who happened to see a piece when he visited a cottage. An inquest was held and it was declared treasure trove and acquired by the British Museum. Within thirty yards of the place were the remains of a Roman villa.

It appears that the field had been ploughed over for generations, and it was not until a tractor plough went that much deeper that the buried hoard came to light. I met the man who had worked the horse plough, and I have never met one so sick at heart as he was at having missed it.

The treasure consisted of some thirty-four pieces of dinner ware, made of silver of a very high standard of purity, dating from about the fourth century A.D. Probably it was acquired gradually, piece by piece, and not as a whole set. From what appear to be Greek inscriptions on the two plates, it may have come from the eastern Mediterranean. Some of the spoons have Christian inscriptions, viz. the Chi-Rho monogram between the letters Alpha and Omega. Evidence of Christianity juxtaposed to very strong paganism, also seen in the Sutton Hoo Ship-Burial, has revolutionized our concept of Christianity in Roman Britain. The official description remarks that "British origin is therefore possible for at least a part of our treasure, and a comparison of the Neptune mask with the Romano-British 'Gorgon' at Bath has led to the suggestion that even the great dish may be a native product. There is, however, little evidence to indicate that any workshop capable of turning out the finer Mildenhall pieces existed in Roman Britain."

The condition of the treasure after such a long period was remarkable, and goes to prove it was buried by its owners in a time of peril and alarm, with the idea of reclaiming it when times were better. But this never happened. However, as the reports state, it escaped mutilation at the hands of barbarian raiders, and has survived some fifteen or sixteen centuries in such perfection that it is felt that the men who made it might still be alive.

Dr. N. F. Hele in his little book on Aldeburgh, published in 1870, tells of finding a ship-burial at Snape. This interesting find was in a tumulus evidently part of an Anglo-Saxon burial ground, because a number of urns were unearthed. He states: "When the whole surface had been exposed, the figure of a boat became evident, the woodwork admitting of only the faintest traces; but the bolts or rivets were laid in parallel rows. The boat was probably flat bottomed and clinker built. It was 48 feet in length, 9 feet 9 inches in width, and 4 feet in depth. In each row of bolts, seven were included within a distance of 3 feet. The rows were six in number on each side and four or five at the bottom of the boat . . . near one end were found some auburn coloured hairs." It was conjectured from this that two persons were so interred rather than one, the hair only being preserved. A gold ring was found, adapted for the thumb, with an oval stone of onyx, or niccolo of a dark colour. It bore the impression of a youth with two ears of bearded corn in one hand and a bowl in the other.

Hele went on to say that from some of the cremated remains found in the vicinity, he considered they were from a race of men of remarkable stature.

There are gaps in the story, it is not all clear and distinct. The Saxons were attacked by the Danes, and it was probably as a consequence that the round towers which are a significant feature of our county, together with Norfolk, came into being. They are of extreme age and appear as though built for defensive purposes. It is rather a happy thought that the Church appropriated them as emblems of peace, building a shrine about them as the one great feature of the village and the landscape. St. Botolph, after whom a number of Suffolk churches are named, carried on the work of Christianizing Suffolk, probably founding his monastery on the banks of the Alde at Iken. So that in time peace flourished, and the formation of the Suffolk character became an established fact.

This brings us to the dialect, the real and natural language of the people. Suffolk, or more strictly speaking East Anglia, is quite rich in its various collections of words and phrases, such as those by Forby, with additions by Spurden and Rye; Nall; FitzGerald in his "Sea Words and Phrases" contributed to the early numbers of the *East Anglian Notes and Queries*; and above all Moor's *Suffolk Words*.

It must be realized, as Walter Rye has pointed out, that some are not dialect words at all in the true sense of the word. Some are merely corruptions, as *sarn* for concern. Others are manufactured words, such as FitzGerald's gamekeeper who referred to a weasel as a *suckeggliest warmint*. Some are merely transpositions of initials as *pulfer* for fulfer (fieldfare), *pample* for trample.

Some of the vowels were used for a multitude of purposes. For instance *A* had to do duty for he, or, our, if, on, at, have, of. An example is its use 'as if': "I'll gi' ye a dunt i the hid, a' ye dew so no more."

'Do', 'don't' are used in a remarkably elliptical sense. "Has the postman called?" "I don't know; du there's no letter fur you." "Shet yin gate, Jim bor, don't them pigs 'll git out." And that remarkable example that appeared recently in the *East Anglian Daily Times*. Someone inquired where the yard broom was and was told, "That stand agin the washus door that do, do that don't, that did."

'Fare' had an infinite variety of meanings. "She fared sick." "They fared angry." "How dew yew fare to feel?" "That don't fare no butter todaa," said of a sickly child.

'That' for it, is still in common use. A splendid example of this is given by Canon Raven in his history of Suffolk. A lady visiting a cottage was alarmed when she saw a tame bird hopping about loose, where was also a cat. "Lor, miss! that 'ont hut that, that that on't," she was told.

'Hold' is another famous word, pronounced 'howd', with a like use of w for l in cold, gold, sold. "Thank-e, sir, I hould right purely," when one is in good health. Or, "She hould vary mahderate," when a person is not at all well. This is used in the same way as agreeing to take just a "drop if yew plaise", when they really mean a jolly good mug full.

Now follow a few examples, some of which are very expressive.
Calimanco Cat. A glossy-skinned, tortoiseshell tabby. This was derived from the old Norwich worsted manufacture of calimanco, which shone like satin.
Canker. The common red field poppy. Otherwise called copper-rose or headache.
Clackbox. The mouth.
Cobweb morning. A misty morning.
Come. A term in churning, "Is the butter come?" "The butter on't come." "Ta een't come."
Company keeper. A lover.
Cow mumble. The cow parsnip. But Cow-tongued was having a tongue smooth one way and rough the other, as purposes served.
Fly time. When flies are troublesome.
Frawn. Frozen. "I'm frawn ta dead a'most."
Frumenty. Wheat boiled in milk, with cinnamon and sugar. This brings forth the apt proverb: "When ta rain frummety, mind ye heen't a dish to seek."
Dutfin for a bridle, belonged exclusively to Suffolk.
Goose-house. A parish cage or lock-up.
Izzard. The last letter of the alphabet.

Julk or *yulk*. A hard blow. "Ta giv em sich a julk ta kill'd em stone dead." Said of a child struck by a windmill sail.

Latch. A most interesting word. A cat latches on its feet when it jumps down; and a latch pan set under a spit catches the fat as it falls.

Long lady. A farthing candle.

Nip. A near split-farthing housewife.

Phiz-gig. A wizened old woman, "tricked out like an old ewe dressed lamb fashion".

Pritch. A sharp-pointed iron instrument such as an eel pritch for catching eels; or a fold-pritch for making holes for hurdles.

Pudding-pye doll. Toad in the hole.

Ringled. Married. But they also ringled pigs.

Sad-bad. Very ill.

Scuppit. A wooden spade made from one piece of wood, handle and spoon. Used for wet work such as cleaning out ditches.

Seed-lep. The box that held the seed when it was broadcast by hand. Anglo-Saxon.

Prah. Pray. "Well, John, how are you?" "Pure well, thanky Sir; prah, how de yeow dew, prah?"

Quake. "Fust toime as iver I see the train, I lay howd on the railings, an' lor I quaked properly."

Wishly. "The children eyed the plum pudding wishly." And this heard at Lavenham in the 1920s, where a young man was seen with a rather large pork pie: "What be you going to dew with thet grut owd pie, bor?" To which he replied, "Bor, I be goin' tew get he into I."

Chill. Another very curious use of a word. They placed a mug of beer before the fire to chill it. That is, to warm it or take off the chill.

Bull's moon. Midnight.

Wem. A defect. I once bought a way-wiser from an old Suffolk dealer, who assured me there wasn't a wem in it. Neither was there.

One cannot write or read of anything in agriculture without coming across a quotation from Tusser's *Five Hundred Points of Good Husbandry*. This was the earliest instance of a book written largely in a provincial dialect, establishing a permanent position in English literature. True he was an Essex man, but he came into Suffolk to farm. This little paragraph comes out of Moor's *Suffolk Words*: "Tusser's work is curious beyond words. The mode of husbandry of his day—about 1550—is very interesting. What a strange thing it is that he relates—not as a piece of information, but as a well-known fact—that in Suffolk wheat never grew."

> In Suffolk again, whereas wheat never grew,
> Good husbandry used, good wheat land I knew—
> This proverb experience long ago gave,
> "That nothing who practiseth, nothing shall have."

Moor also speaks of the alteration of place names, such as East Bergholt to Barfel, Burgh to Bath, Bruisyard to Bridjit, Dunningworth to Dunnafer, Grundisburgh to Grundsburra, Lowestoft to Laystiff, Monewden to Mulladen, Waldringfield to Wanaful.

Gile's Trip to London, published in 1871, is considered one of the best narratives given in dialect, of which I give an extract:

I set down, and nothin' pertickler happened arter that till we got to a place about ten mile fudder on. There we stopped a few minutes, and a pleasant-luking, middle-aged man with a twinkle in his eye goes round and lukes in the carriage an ses in a serious solemn woice, jest as if he wor givin' out tew lines of a hymn long mater at a Methodist Chapel—

"Chaange here for Bury, Thurston, and Elmswell;
Elmswell, Thurston and Bury, chaange here!"

Presently he coms to my carriage, and he lukes in and he gives out the tew lines.

I ses, "Du you pertickler want me to chaange here for them places?" He put his hand on my showder and ses, "Whare are ye goin' tu?"

"Lunnon," I ses.

"Then," he ses, "Yow set still, hev patience, and yow'll be thare—some time or other," and he tips me a wink, larfs, and walks off, to guv out the saame tew lines in every one o' the carriages.

The Rivers

While the rivers shall run to ocean, while the shadows shall move in the mountain valleys, while the sky shall feed the stars, always shall thy honour, and thy name, and thy glory abide.

Virgil.

Suffolk is almost entirely surrounded by water and there is no doubt but that its numerous rivers have contributed greatly to its beauty as a county, as also to its prosperity. It is bounded on the north by the Waveney, in the south by the Stour, with the Linnet and the Lark on the west dividing it from Cambridge. Then there come such lovely streams as the Orwell and Brett in the south, the Deben, the Alde, with the Blyth. All the rivers flow eastward to the sea, except the minor streams of the Little Ouse, the Lark and the Linnet, and the Brett. One peculiarity is that several of these rivers change name, such as the Gipping which turns into the Orwell at Ipswich; the Yox which rises at Laxfield, becomes the Min or Minsmere when it reaches Yoxford, and the Alde becomes the Ore at Sudbourne.

The Waveney (Anglo-Saxon Wafien, 'waving or troubled water') is the largest, and perhaps the most beautiful. It rises at South Lopham, near Diss, in swampy ground, within a stone's throw of the Little Ouse; and whereas the one flows east the other flows west. The Waveney crosses into Suffolk at Stuston. In many respects the river is like a country lane, as its Saxon name suggests, and meanders about in a remarkable manner, now through broad measures, now past rushy flats, drainage mills and slopes of heath. For example when it reaches Bungay it suddenly makes a northwards loop of 3½ miles, before it touches the town a second time some 500 to 600 yards away. At Hoxne it is joined by the Dove which rises at nearby Yaxley, after which it flows

Snape Maltings on the River Alde

under the Golden Bridge, redolent of St. Edmund's martyrdom. (This event, by the way, was known in old Suffolk parlance as Deadman's Day, 20th November.) Alongside the stream are many beautiful willow- and poplar-lined stretches, with peaceful marshlands, grazings for red poll cattle; and old world villages such as Palgrave and Botesdale, which latter was once a great coaching thoroughfare, its name derived from St. Botolph. Incidentally, the old marshmen dried the heads of the huge bulrushes and rubbed them up to stuff pillows and cushions.

At the beginning of the century the Waveney was navigable by wherry up as far as Bungay staith, 15 miles. Long years ago it must have been possible to get up even farther, for an anchor was found in the bed of the little tributary at Weybread; and in 1818 a meeting was held at Yarmouth to discuss a plan for extending navigation to Diss, but nothing came of it.

> You've heard of Old Bungay,—her fam'd Navigation,—
> Her Waveney, the pride and delight of her Town;—
> That brings to her Wharf the choice wares of the Nation;
> And adds every year to her wealth and renown.
> You've heard too of Diss, and her Duck-Pond of puddle;
> Her Mere, fam'd for mud, and of reptiles the den;—
> You've heard of Diss Beer, which we drink,—and not fuddle
> Of her Ginger-bread Cakes and her Diss-honest Men!
> And now you shall hear how these Diss-honest fellows,
> Have a project to make us all wonder and stare;
> 'Tis to steal all the Trade from Old Bungay,—they tell us—
> By joining Diss Pond to the Waveney and Yare.
>
> 1820.

The wherry, it might be mentioned, took the place of the old keels at the early part of the last century. Whereas the mast of the keel was stepped nearly amidships, that of the wherries was placed within a few feet of the bows. The wherries were staffed by a man and a boy. When they went gliding by, they fitted into the landscape and were the prettiest sight possible. They had broad graceful lines, with bright colours on their bows, like barges on the canals, and a shining weather vane at their mast-head, and were the most weatherly craft in the world. With huge sails of a rich madder, they towered above the alders and the willows making as fair a picture as it was possible to see. They were handled with ease by a race of men who understood them completely, as though they were human. Naturally enough these wherrymen knew every reach along the course, such as the Shipmeadow Shoals, Old Molls' Lock, Roast Beef Corner and the like. Parts of the river were noted for pike, and a stuffed pike was said to be food for the gods.

H. M. Doughty, squire of Theberton, wrote a delightful little book, published in 1897, under the title *Summer in Broadland*. When their wherry got up to Bungay, they had to manoeuvre it to turn round. He wrote:

Cows were feeding round the ship, and the "whish" and "coop-a-wee" [direction to horses] of ploughmen, came from a near hillside.

Just as we were seeking a wide place to turn in, a labourer came to look at us. He had been 'fying-out' [cleaning] a ditch holl.

"That fare whooly stammin how yow got yar pleasure ship up hinwai [hither]. I've wrought a good tidy time on this here mashes, but blame me, if I iver see the likes of yow afore."

When he was 10 years old the poet Crabbe was sent by his father as a boarder to Bungay grammar school. He spent his first night thinking about his mother. In the morning he whispered to his bed fellow, "Master G, can you put on your shirt? for I'm afraid I cannot."

Whilst here he was placed in a large dog kennel for punishment, known as the 'black hole'. The place was crammed and poor Crabbe was nearly suffocated. He shrieked out, and at last out of desperation bit the hand of the boy next to him. So the cry went up, "Crabbe is dying: Crabbe is dying!" and the door was opened.

Beccles (Beclyssen, 'enclosed') and the river seemed to be made for one another, because they have lived together for many a century, and here grew up the old couplet that must have been made by an early Edward Lear:

> To Beccles, to Beccles, to buy a bunch of nettles:
> Home again, home again,—What's o'clock Basset?

The old billyboy ketches used to put in here laden with coal from Newcastle, or some other commodity from London, or to take out a cargo. The old town, with its old-world houses, creeps down to the river, not forgetting the gardens, while the church tower, standing all by itself, looks quietly on. From this point of view some of the finest sunset effects in Suffolk can be seen, and that is saying something.

The church with its noble south porch saw the uniting of the Reverend Edmund Nelson and Catherine Suckling, who were to become the parents of our Lord Nelson. They were married 11th May 1749. Then on 15th December 1783 our poet Crabbe, after a long courtship, married his 'Mira', otherwise Sarah Elmy. The Ringers have one of those huge jugs, made locally and bearing the inscription:

> When I am filled with liquor strong,
> Each man drink once, and then ding-dong.
> Drink not too much to cloud your knobs
> Lest you forget to make the Bobs.

In 1972 the 150-foot tower of the fifteenth-century church was sold to the borough council for £1. The council had to assume legal ownership to be able to spend money on its restoration.

It is a pleasant voyage down the river, taking one reach after another. You might expect it to go out to sea over Oulton Broad, but it turns away in a loop round Lothingland before it meets the Yare and submerges its identity in the calm beauty of Breydon Water. However, there is a cut or narrow channel, called Lyke Dyke by the old wherrymen.

Camden says that the Waveney flowed out to sea through Oulton Broad and Lake Lothing, making a sea port at Kirkley. But the North Sea with its downwards thrust by the north-east winds, made a bar of sand and shingle across the mouth, so that the river changed direction and went round by Lothingland, leaving the south-east point of Norfolk projecting into the marshes. This is now returned to Norfolk under the new county boundaries scheme. This will include the famous Burgh Castle, which in Camden's time was "quite overgrown with briars and thorns, among which they now and then dig up Roman coins". Burgh Castle was the scene of one of the best of the early inland water frolics.

The Blyth ('pleasant river'), is probably the most historic of the Suffolk rivers. because its mouth once formed the port of Dunwich, the ancient capital of East Anglia. It rises at Laxfield in High Suffolk and flows through such old-world places as Ubbeston, which was of Danish origin. One senses the antiquity of these fields, so redolent of Roman times. At Heveningham the river widens out into a lake, setting the scene for Heveningham Hall, Wyatt's masterpiece, and then goes on to Walpole and Halesworth (Healesuurda, probably 'Hael's farm'). From then to Blyford and Blythburgh, and so to the sea at Walberswick (Walberdeswyk, 'Walhbert's village'). In its course of only 20 miles it traverses Roman country and Roman highways, because a statuette of Venus was found near Blyford bridge (one of those old hump-backed variety as was at Snape)*. The river was navigable as far as Halesworth, and the old billyboy ketches used to ply thither in the days of sail.

There were four locks—at Bulcamp, Blyford, Mells and Halesworth—and there was a quay at Blyford as well as at Halesworth. By about 1850 there were at least a dozen wherries working this way, and their memory is perpetuated today by the Wherry Inn in Quay Street, exhibiting a very nicely painted sign. But the continual blocking of Southwold Harbour put a stop to these activities. Halesworth was a very busy little agricultural market town with numerous maltings and iron works producing agricultural implements.

The view of the Blythburgh valley from Blythburgh is one of the most peaceful and pastoral scenes possible, with Henham Woods as a background to the north, and the heronry near the track of the old Southwold railway. George Gissing when retired to his cottage in Devonshire, and dreaming of past English summers, recalled the scene: "The stream ripples and glances over its brown bed warmed with sunbeams, by its bank the green flags wave and rustle, and all about the meadows shine in pure gold of buttercups. The hawthorn hedges are a mass of gleaming blossom, which scents the breeze. There above rises the heath, yellow-mantled with gorse, and beyond, if I walk for an hour or two, I shall come upon the sandy cliffs of Southwold, and look over the northern sea." It was not by chance that the beautiful Blythburgh church was planted on its banks, or that this part of

* The hump-backed bridge at Snape was rebuilt in 1959, see page 58.

England has been the home and haunts of artists since the days of Constable.

The old railway was so intimately connected with the river, that its route must have been almost Arcadian. Beyond Blythburgh bridge came a marvellous vista of the river estuary and the track lay through reedy backwaters until it reached Walberswick Common, aflame with heather and gorse. Beyond the station the line dropped down to the swing bridge, a classical piece of engineering, which consisted of a bowstring girder that turned on a steel caisson sunk in the river bed.

Remains of the ill-fated plane in which Lieutenant Joseph Kennedy, brother of John F. Kennedy, lost his life on 12th August 1944, were found in 1972 in a wood near Blythburgh. The explosion caused a great scare in local villages and two of my children on holiday from school, together with others from Westleton, scampered off to investigate but never reached the scene.

At Wenhaston, famous for its Doom, an Alice Bakon ('Wedowe', 1510) in her will directed that her "Body to be buried in St. Peter's churchyard, my soul to God an our lady St. Mary and all saints—to high altar of Wenhaston for tithes forgotten xijd.—two skeppes with bees and the waxe thereof coming, the one half to have light afore the Image of our Lady St. Mary, and the other afore the Image of St. Peter." Beeswax was used for making candles.

In 1967 some 1,200 acres of heathland, marshes and woods near Walberswick were designated as a nature reserve. Most of the land has been in the Blois family for some 300 years, and it was through the generosity of the then owner, Sir Charles Blois, some of this heathland was once used as sheep walks, amongst them Tinkers' Walks and part of the route of the old Southwold railway.

Westwood Marshes are also included. They contain one of the biggest reed beds in England, and are the home of several species of marshland birds. They were formerly drained and used for grazing, but were flooded in 1940 to form an anti-invasion obstacle. Since then they have become overgrown with reeds that now cover the entire area.

The Nature Conservancy has bought 95 acres of tidal mud

flats on the Blyth at Blythburgh. These are known rather
delightfully as the Angel Marshes. In a statement the Conservancy
says their heaths are covered with heather, bracken and sand
sedge, with occasional clumps of gorse and broom. This is a type
of vegetation which was once common on the Suffolk coast but
is now steadily disappearing through afforestation and the demands
of agriculture. Since the rabbit population has declined young trees
have sprung up, but it is hoped to restore these heathlands to their
native state, with the characteristic bird, plant and insect life.

The Alde rises at Brundish near Framlingham, where in 1879
the parish clerk delighted in the name of Alderman Stopher. It
flows via Bruisyard, Rendham, Snape and Iken to the coast, where
it suddenly takes a right-angled bend at Slaughden at within a
hundred yards of the sea, and flows out some 10 miles further south
at Hollesley Bay.

As recently as 1896 at Slaughden there were eight houses occupied by about thirty people, and several warehouses were to be
found there and trades carried on. Slaughden may be taken as
the beginning of the bar proper.

In many respects the Alde is a lovely river, with certain most
interesting aspects, and has evoked rather opposite or contrary
emotions. For instance, John Freeman wrote thus of it:

> How near I walked to Love
> How long, I cannot tell.
> I was like the Alde that flows
> Quietly through green level lands,
> So quietly, it knows
> Their shape, their greenness and their shadows well;
> And then undreamily for miles it goes
> And silently beside the sea.

And this is how Crabbe described it:

> Here samphire banks and saltweed bound the flood
> Here stake and seaweed withering in the mud;
> And higher up a ridge of all things base,
> Which some strong tide has roll'd upon the place.

(Incidentally, the site of Crabbe's cottage is now under the waves.)

Robert Reyce in his *Breviary of Suffolk* has a characteristic description of the scene, which was in his day called the Fromas.

As we do descend loward into the inward of the country wee do find another special ryver called of old time Fromas who, making his beginning at Tattingstone and Framlingham, desendeth to Marlesford and so south east of Farneham entertayneth another ryver called the Gleme, which cometh from Rendlesham and both the Glemhams thus passing forth to Snape bridge it Embraceth another river coming from Carlton by Saxmundham, and so continuing his course by Iken receiveth a third small brooke, with all which accompanied it fetcheth a great compass towards Aldeburgh and Sudbourne, at this length dedicates it self into the broad see at Orford. So likewise nott far of another current flows from Chillesford and Butley doth here hide itself in the deep sea.

At Snape bridge (Snape, 'a boggy place') the river ceases to be tidal. This old humped-backed structure, with its reflection mirrored in the water, centuries old, was demolished in 1959 owing to the exigencies of modern traffic. It marked the limit to which the barges could sail, commemorated by the inspired inn sign, 'The Plough and Sail'. At Iken Cliff the river fans out almost into a lake, making a picturesque setting amid lush meadows surrounded by trees. Indeed, Iken is an interesting spot, both by name and nature. The church standing on a knoll overlooking the river is one of those dedicated to the elusive St. Botolph, and it has been conjectured that here was the spot Ikanhoe, where he built his monastery. It may well have been so.

Near here is a field called Camping Close, redolent of that barbaric game of early football, which was really a shin-kicking match.

From Iken we reach Slaughden, which once had a quay, and luggers plied from thence to London, including the *Unity*—owned by the Groomes—that took Crabbe to London to make his fortune. And from there, by the same means, so many local folk travelled to the Great Exhibition of 1851. It was this exhibition that almost brought London to a standstill and emptied the shops, making a profit of £186,000. It is good to know that the Royal Commission for the Exhibition of 1851 still functions.

Aldeburgh is noted for its mile-long Crag Path, and when

Walter White was thereabouts in 1865 he was told by a fisherman that the navvies made it after they had done building the railway.

Orford (Oreford, 'ford at the shore'), cut off from the sea by the shingle bank, has deteriorated gracefully from a franchised borough returning two Members to Parliament, to a village. Its church is noble, and nobler still the keep of the castle, built by Henry II as a foil to his dissident barons. Continuing down we come to Havergate Island and the avocets, to the Butley river, which is a tributary stream of the Alde that flows through historic ground and leads one to the abbey founded so long ago by Ranulph de Glanville, who was known as the 'King's Eye'. Butley, too, figures in that local classic of *Margaret Catchpole*, wherein Captain Bargood sets his henchmen to work on smuggling, when not otherwise employed. So the Alde, now known as the Ore, flows out into the sea by Shingle Street, which is one of the most desolate, but interesting tracts of coast and one of those intriguing names to be met with, that speaks for itself of great antiquity.

The Deben (Debyn, 'the steep or headlong') rises at Debenham and is another of Suffolk's charming and historic streams. It flows on gently and peacefully through a varying landscape of woodland, marsh and heathland. Never very wide it is spanned by sundry one-arched bridges ere it reaches Woodbridge where it is tidal, passing such pleasant places as Brandeston, Hoo, Letheringham, Easton, Ufford; and thence by Rendlesham, Waldringfield and Ramsholt to Bawdsey Haven, and so to the sea. On the right bank two small tributaries joined in one from Clopton and Ashbocking add to the volume of the water. Just before Woodbridge it is joined by the Finn. Of its usefulness and antiquity it is said that no less than fifteen medieval watermills were at work along its banks.

A trip down the river for geologists provides an interesting study, with a fine section of red crag at Ramsholt and Bawdsey, and the re-deposited coralline crag at Ramsholt and Sutton. Coprolite was raised at Waldringfield, washed on the bank, and then taken away in barges. Just at the mouth of the river occurs an outcrop of the London Clay.

FitzGerald loved the river, the stretches from Woodbridge which he knew so well, having spent the whole of his life in or

about the little town. "The dear old Deben, with the worthy cutter sloop going forth into the world as the sun sinks." He loved the riverside hamlets with their churches, the tawny heathlands and the farmhouse at Sutton Haugh where he often smoked a pipe with his friend Alfred Smith.

To modern archaeologists the river has taken on a new meaning, because it must have been along its quiet waters that the 14-foot beamed ship, or barge, rowed by thirty-eight oarsmen, was ferried for the ship-burial at Sutton Hoo, presumably from Bawdsey Haven. It was then manhandled to its resting place over the heath as a cenotaph for a warrior king.

Then hundreds of years later, it was at Bawdsey Haven, then known as Gooseford, and so called until the eighteenth century, that the local ships of Edward III's navy collected together before they sailed for Calais. The fleet was then ordered to sail to Swine-humber, which was evidently near Yarmouth. Here they met other ships from the north and returned to the Orwell for the king to embark. This grouping is still perpetuated in the name of Kingsfleet for a sheet of water that spreads out beside the stream. When the Westminster Abbey effigies were being restored after having been damaged by water in 1941, a full-length figure of Edward III showed that he was left-handed, although his penmanship was of great note.

Wilford Hollows is the name given to a valley that divides what was known as the Sands district from the Claylands. This drops down from what was the gorse-covered Sutton Walks (Walks, 'sheep walks'), now cultivated. It is a particularly lovely glen, studded with oaks, and the banks are bright with wild flowers. Here also the lapwings give vent to their plaintive cry, while the waters of the Deben flow silently on.

At Melton in this hollow the former Primitive Methodist chapel, built in 1860, was a year later removed bodily a distance of 18 feet, by means of bottle jacks. So that sort of thing was done long before they thought of moving Ballingdon Hall 1,000 yards uphill.

Woodbridge, noted for its sunsets, has been always an attractive little town, in spite of the fact that FitzGerald called his yacht *Scandal* because he said that was its staple product. It climbs up the side of a hill, topped by the market place and its old tower mill. The church approach is lined by pollarded willows.

The Tide Mill, Woodbridge, on the River Deben

In the peacefulness of yesterday, the first house on the Ipswich side was named Alpha Cottage, and the last house on the way out was appropriately Omega Cottage. This seems to suggest a tight, compact little township shut in from the busy world, another Cranford. Its old Tide Mill, now seeking restoration, was granted to the priory by Sir Robert Willoughby in 1436; and at the Dissolution it was so disposed to Sir John Wingfield in 1539.

The quay was always busy, and all kinds of commodities were loaded and unloaded, such as timber, bricks, and especially butter and cheese, which Defoe duly noted. There were extensive salt-works here for the fishing trade, and in the latter part of the eighteenth century there was a potash warehouse, bearing the appropriate name Potash House. California Cottages, so called in 1881, were probably named because of their remote position. This would apply to that district thus denominated now.

Bernard Barton became known as the 'Woodbridge Poet', and his neat little house in Cumberland Street still presents a smiling Georgian frontal, and bears his name—Barton's Cottage. Like other writers, especially poets, before and since, he rather wanted to devote his life to literature and so escape from the confines of his desk in Alexander's Bank. He complained of bodily discomfort, so this is what Charles Lamb sent him by way of advice: "You are too apprehensive about your complaints. . . . Believe the general sense of the mercantile world, which holds that desks are not deadly. It is the mind good B.B. and not the limbs, that faint by long sittings. Think of the patience of tailors—think how long the Lord Chancellor sits, think of the brooding hen."

He lies in the little graveyard of the Friends' Meeting House in Turn Lane, under the simple inscription:

> Bernard Barton,
> died
> 19 of 2 mo. 1849
> Aged 65.

It was said of him:

> His virtue walked the narrow road,
> Nor made a pause nor left a void,
> And sure the Eternal Master found
> His simple talent well employed.

And surely this old Deben was not unknown to smuggling, with its creeks and outlets so ready for the purpose. Such for instance as Falkenham, where the river is approached down that sloping village street overhung with giant cedar trees, until one comes across an inn known as 'The Dog'. Tradition has it that this was a venue for run goods, because from an upper window there is a clear view to Ramsholt church and its oval-shaped tower, alleged to have been used by the free men.

The Orwell is one of those peculiar rivers that begins life as the Gipping rising at Mendlesham Green, and then after giving its name to Ipswich, passes under a bridge there and comes out as the Orwell. It is moreover the most lyrical of all the Suffolk rivers. One would think that the Waveney or the Deben would have caused poets to burst into song, but not so. In the parish of Freston the river was referred to as 'The Water'. They had never heard of the Orwell.

> Meandering Gippin, loveliest stream,
>   That ever roll'd its limpid flood
> Through many a rich sequestered mead,
>   And many an overhanging wood.
>
> I owe thee much; thy gentle tide
>   Deserves what I can ne'er bestowe,
> To flow along immortal lines
>   As sweetly as thy waters flow.

In the upper reaches it glides through such places at Stow-market, where it is lined by old industrial walls. Here are memories of Milton's pupilage under the pious Dr. Youngs and the mulberry tree that was planted in the rectory garden. Here too you will find the Abbots' Hall Folk Museum that is so full of Suffolk yesterdays.

Needham Market comes next, where to the delight of every-one, and especially railway lovers, the station has been reopened. It was closed under the Beeching 'axe', this pleasant bit of railway Gothic, and, through public-spirited action by the Gipping Rural Council and the Needham Market Parish Council, it is the first station in the country to be re-embodied into regular service.

I wonder what happened when the station was first opened. Probably there were a lot of flags and bunting about, there might even have been a daguerreotype taken to delineate the bearded company that brought it into action. Certain it is that the re-opening provided a real gala day. Needless to say, the first train on that occasion was late. Over 100 people turned up for the great event, and two extra coaches had been added to the 8 a.m. from Cambridge, but it was six minutes late pulling into the station. However, there was one thing not specially recorded in this reopening, the sort of thing that did not happen at the first opening. Bottles of champagne (vintage not known) were presented to the driver and the guard, and photographs were taken. One can be quite sure that did not happen when Needham Market station was new and the railway world was young.

The Orwell, which is best seen at high water, since it is really an estuary of the sea, is very beautiful. At low tide it has rather wide banks of mud. It is one of the famous rivers mentioned by Drayton in his *Polyolbion*:

> For Orwell comming in from Ipswich thinks that shee
> Should stand for it with Stour, and lastly they agree,
> That since the Britons hence their first discoveries made,
> And that into the East they first were taught to trade,
> Besides of all the Roads and Havens of the East,
> This Harbour where they meet is reckoned for the best.

Robert Reyce, writing in his *Breviary* of 1618, gives this quaint description: "The last river on this side, is this Vre who taking his source about Bacton runneth to Stour, beneath the which after it hath received the brookes coming from Rattlesden and One-house, it hasteneth to Needham, Blakenham, Bramford, Ipswich receiving beneath Stoke south from Ipswich the Chatsham Water and Belstead thus never ceaseth until it drowneth it selfe in the bottomless well in the mouth of the Haven named of old from the said ryver Vrewell haven, butt in these dayes Orewell haven."

Moreover, it was one of Constable's rivers. He must have walked and rode along its banks, or navigated some of its reaches. One of his pictures, *View on the Orwell, at Ipswich,* is in the Victoria and Albert Museum.

As we go downstream, taking the north bank, the first thing

Breckland

Guildhall at Eye : the best preserved of the early sixteenth–century guild
houses of Suffolk

The Orangery at Heveningham Hall

Gainsborough's House at Sudbury

Temple in Euston Hall Park

The primeval forest of Staverton Park

Martello Tower at Aldeburgh: now a holiday home administered by the Landmark Trust

The former Neptune Inn, Ipswich

On the edge of Rendlesham Forest

Kings Fleet

to note is Holy Wells. The name, an ancient one, originated from the numerous springs which break out from the junction of the crag strata and the London Clay. These springs are mentioned in Taylor's *Monasticus* as being much resorted to by pilgrims. The rising ground is Hog Highland, which rises from the north-east shore up towards Gainsborough Lane. Bourne Bridge, an ancient brick structure, carries the old road over the stream.

Cresting the high ground above Hog Highland is Gainsborough Lane. This once bore the soft scenery that Gainsborough loved, and was a favourite sketching ground of the artist. Much of the scenery hereabouts was introduced into his pictures, including "The Market Cart" in the National Gallery. Not far removed is Alnesbourne Priory, now Priory Farm, associated with Charles II, with a supposed secret passage to the Ancient House, Ipswich. Now comes Orwell Park, with its water tower and observatory. This was originally the residence of the celebrated Admiral Vernon, who gained the empiric victory of Portobello. That eccentric and litigious character, Colonel George Tomline, became possessed of this in 1873, and much extended its 200 acres.

Broke Hall, which comes next, commemorates the name of Phillip Broke, who commanded the *Shannon* in the historic fight with the *Chesapeake* in Boston Bay in 1813. Opposite is Butterman's Bay, the deepest part of the river.

On the south bank the first to note is Wherstead Park. Then comes the famous red-bricked Freston Tower, the village of which delights in an inn called the 'Freston Boot'.

Of the tower it might be related that in 1730, 11th April, an advertisement appeared in the *Ipswich Journal*: "To be Lett ready Furnished. The Mansion House call'd Freston Tower, three miles off Ipswich, containing a large Hall, three Parlours, four Chambers, two large Garretts, a good Kitchen, Brewing Office and Utensils, two Cellars, a large Orchard, Garden, Stables, and Pasture for a Horse in Summer. Enquire of Mr. Thomas Grimwood, Linen Draper, in Ipswich."

This tower was also used for smallpox patients, 1772-9, and as early as 1767 the following advertisement appeared in the same journal: "Mr. Sutton of Ingatestone informs the public that he has fitted up Freston Tower House for the reception of patients under Inocculation. General terms for patients—six, four and three guineas."

There was also a bit of folk-lore about the place, because an old rhyme concerned Ipswich couples.

> No burgess on his wedding day,
> Which falls in whitethorn merry May,
> Shall happy be, in house or bower,
> Who does not visit Freston Tower.

The Cat House, noted in *Margaret Catchpole* as a smugglers' device, is halfway between Freston and Chelmondiston.

Woolverstone Park, once the home of the Berners' family, spreads its green carpet to the water's edge. In the grounds is an obelisk, 96 feet high, topped by a globe and dated 1793—"To the memory of the best of fathers".

Pin Mill comes next, with its inn of 'Butt and Oyster' on the hard, and its memories of smuggling days and barge races. Many of the famous Thames barges were built here. It is reputed to have been so named from a rich landowner conferring on his daughter as pin money the proceeds of the windmills hereabouts. Mills then yielded a capital and were a never-failing source of income. Chelmondiston is on the high ground above.

On this reach of the river lived Thomas Colson, also better known as 'Robinson Crusoe', in a crazy craft of his own making. His career is recounted in the book of Suffolk folk-lore. Under the title of the "Ancient Fisherman", Mrs. Cobbold indited one of her dreary poems. He was a firm believer in the evil agency of wizards and witchcraft. On this subject he was by no means uninformed. His mind was so haunted by the dreams of charms and enchantments, as to fancy he was continually under the influence of these mischievous tormentors. His arms and legs, and almost his whole body was encircled with the bones of horses, rings, amulets and verses, words, etc., as spells and charms to protect him against their evil devices. When talking with him, he would describe how he could see them hovering about his person, and endeavouring by their arts to punish and torment him. He was constantly being warned to leave his old craft, but he would not. He considered his charms were effective, but being driven on the mud bank by a violent storm on 3rd October 1811 he was seen and implored to come ashore. But he would not and went down with his contraption. He gained a livelihood by fishing.

Before the coming of the railways, the whole of the coal trade between Newcastle and London was in the hands of the owners of vessels belonging to Ipswich. These vessels were called Ipswich Cats, being of large tonnage and standing very high above the water.

On the 14th August 1828 a whale was found on the sands at Harwich and towed up the Orwell as far as Bourne Bridge. Its skeleton was for many years in the Ipswich Mechanics' Institution.

It is said that Queen Elizabeth I sailed down the Orwell in 1561, whereas Queen Elizabeth II landed at Shotley Point when she visited Ipswich in 1961 just 400 years later. We might end this trip down the Orwell with Bernard Barton's poem:

Sweet stream! on whose banks in my childhood residing,
    Untutor'd by life in the lessons of care;
In the heart-cheering whispers of hope still confiding,
    Futurity's prospects seem'd smiling and fair.

Dear river! how gaily the sun-beams are glancing
    On the murmuring waves, as they roll to the main!
While my tempest-tost bark, on life's ocean advancing,
    Despairs of e'er finding a harbour again.

Fair *Orwell!* those banks which thy billows are laving,
    Full oft have I thoughtlessly saunter'd along;
Or beneath those tall trees, which the fresh breeze is waving,
    Have listen'd with rapture to nature's wild song.

But say, can thy groves, though with harmony ringing,
    Recall the emotions of youthful delight?
Or can thy gay banks, where the flowerets are springing,
    Revive the impressions they once could excite?

Ah no! Those bright visions for ever are vanish'd,
    Thy fairy dominion, sweet Fancy, is o'er;
The soft soothing whispers of Hope too are banish'd,
    The "Song of the Syrens" enchants me no more.

Adieu, lovely Orwell! for ages still flowing!
  On thy banks may the graces, and virtues combine:
Long, long may thy beauties, fresh raptures bestowing,
Diffuse the sweet pleasures they've yielded to mine.

When this head is reclined on its last clay-cold pillow,
  My memory forgotten, my name passed away;
May a Minstrel, more bless'd, snatch my harp from the willow
  And devote to thee, *Orwell!* a worthier lay.

The Stour has the distinction of being the broader river, dividing Suffolk from Essex on its entire southern boundary. It rises from three sources—the first at Kedington in Suffolk, the second at Cambridgeshire, and the third at Essex—and its entire length is some 50 miles; with three principal Suffolk tributaries of the Glem, the Box and the Brett. These rivulets unite about 7 or 8 miles from their respective springs. In its progress the chief places are Clare, Long Melford and Sudbury, not a bad lot by any standard. It has been described as the Queen of the Suffolk waters, both in regards to scenery and the area drained, which is chiefly on the Suffolk side.

It was one of the chief inlets for various invaders, such as the Saxons and the Danes, who found easy access to the interior. Moreover, one must not forget that it flows through the charming vale of Dedham, as also such bays as Seafield, Holbrook and Erwarton, all of great beauty, enough to inspire such painters as Gainsborough and Constable, who were both born on its banks. When it reaches Manningtree it is 2 miles wide. Its course is then about 12 miles in a direct line to Harwich.

When Defoe reached Harwich in 1722, he sent his horses round by Manningtree—"where there is a timber bridge over the Stour, called Cattawade Bridge". As for himself he went up the Orwell to Ipswich. But he had this to say: "A traveller will hardly understand me, especially a seaman, when I speak of the river Stour and the river Orwell for they know them by no other names than that of Manningtree Water and Ipswich Water." Cattawade Bridge, it might be mentioned, is a hamlet of Brantham and Thomas Tusser lived at Brantham Hall.

Sudbury is the chief town described by the old chronicler as "an ancient towne seated on the Stower, over which it has a fair bridge leading into Essex". The original bridge, or what was supposed to be the original, was carried away by a flood on the 4th November 1520, but was restored the following year. Dr Taylor passed over it in 1515, in the custody of the sheriff on his way to the stake at Hadleigh.

Gainsborough was born in the parish of St. Gregory, and this is what Sir Joshua Reynolds said of him: "If ever this nation should produce genius sufficient to acquire us the honourable distinction of an English School, the name of Gainsborough will be transmitted to posterity in the history of the art, among the very first of that rising name."

> Mourn, Painting, mourn, recline thy drooping head,
>   And fling thy useless pallet [*sic*] on the ground!
> Gainsborough is numbered with the silent dead,
>   And plaintive sighs from hills and vales resound.
>
> His genius lov'd his country's native views,
>   Its taper spires, green lawns, and shelter'd farms:
> He touch'd each scene with nature's genuine hues,
>   And gave the English Landscape all its charms.
>
> Who now shall paint mild evening's tranquil hours,
>   The cattle slow returning from the plain,
> The glow of sultry noon, the transient show'r,
>   The dark brown furrows rich with golden grain?
>
> Who shall describe the cool sequester'd spot,
>   Where winding riv'lets through the willows glide;
> Or paint the manners of the humble cot,
>   Where meek content and poverty reside?
>
>   (From the *Suffolk Garland*, 1788, author unknown)

I must confess to an enjoyment of Walter White's description of his walk to Sudbury from Waldringfield. He asked a man how they felt after the disfranchisement: "... 'taint easy to say how we feels. Some thinks we ought to be lookin' up a bit since the town made the trimmin's for the Princess Royal's weddin' dresses."

And so we come to Shotley Spit and intriguing Erwarton,

both by name and the curious gatehouse. At the house Anne
Boleyn is said to have stayed and left her heart behind. The church
is of great interest because of the Davillers' tombs, one of which
shows a cross-legged knight the earliest effigy of its kind. He was
probably Sir Bartholomew Davillers who died in 1287. Nearby
is a haunted lane, which brought forth a verse by the late
A. C. C. Hervey:

> Down on the marsh he lived, or stood, or died—
> How many years or centuries ago?
> And why just there? Was blood upon his hands?
> Or had he loved in vain? This tale of clown,
> Felon, lover, will nevermore be known.
> And yet—I like you, Johnny All Alone.

But we must mention the little rivers, such as the Dove, which
has its source near Mendlesham, or Frog Hall at Finningham. Its
chief and only town is Eye. At the village of Thorndon, it divides,
and the second tributary passes southward in the direction of
Stowmarket. Amongst the trees the village of Wetheringsett
hides and holds the river which passes through, a truly delightful
stream, purling beneath a series of little bridges. Richard Hakluyt
was rector in 1590, and there wrote his famous *Voyages*.

The Lark, which more or less divides Suffolk from Cambridgeshire, rises near Bradfield Combust. Just beyond the old jail at
Bury, it is joined by a miniature stream, the Linnet, which rises
in Ickworth Park, and runs to Mildenhall, where it is lost in the
Fens. For many years during the last century Bury St. Edmunds
and Mildenhall were supplied with coal and other heavy goods
by means of the Lark. At Bury, barges left the river near Fornham
St. Martin Church, entered an artificial cut (still known as the
'Coal River'), and were unloaded at a wharf against the old
maltings on the Mildenhall Road.

3

The Suffolk Coast

We are as near to heaven by sea as by land!

Hakluyt's *Voyages*

Suffolk is essentially a maritime county, with its eastern borders of some 50 miles on the North Sea. Moreover, Lowestoft Ness is the most easterly point in England, with another at Orford Ness. Although there are no great indentations in this coastline it has suffered from the encroachment of the sea along the whole length from Gunton in the north to Landguard in the south.

A number of sandbanks lie off the coast, such as the Cork Ledge and the Cork Knoll off Felixstowe; the Cutter Sand and the Kettle Bottom off Bawdsey; together with the Bawdsey Bank and the Shipwash. Between Orford Ness and Thorpe Ness are the Ridge and the Gabbard, while further north is the Sizewell Bank. Then comes the Barnard off Kessingland, and the Newcome and the Holme off Lowestoft; while between Corton and Gorleston lies the Corton Sand. Sixty-two buoys have been placed between Harwich Harbour and the Yare, but they have to be moved occasionally because of shifting sand.

In addition to the buoys there were four lightships, namely the Cork, the Shipwash, the Outer Gabbard and the Corton lightships. After 128 years of service the Cork lightship off Felixstowe, with its crew of eleven, seven of whom were on board at any one time, has been replaced by a large automatic unmanned navigation buoy, Lansby. The first lightship at the Cork Sand was towed into position in April 1844. Shifting banks and the improvements to the main ship channel forced changes in its station. The cost of maintenance had reached £30,000 a year, and although each 40 feet Lansby costs £150,000, the maintenance is not expected to exceed £3,000.

The Suffolk coast was the first to be systematically lighted, commencing at Lowestoft, when in 1609 the Corporation of Trinity House erected a pair of lights for the direction of ships through the dangerous Stanford Channel. These were known as the High Light and the Low Light.

The High Light was open at the top when first built, and a coal fire was kept blazing at night. This fire caused a good deal of damage to surrounding property. This early light was superseded in 1676 by a brick and stone lighthouse, which bore the legend: "Erected by the Brotherhood of Trinity House of Deptford Strond in the Mastership of Samuel Pepys Esq., Secretary to the Admiralty of England, A.D. 1676." It was 40 feet high and 20 in diameter. The plaque is still preserved in the present structure. In 1777, according to Gillingwater, owing to the decay of the upper part of the tower, it was decided to remove the top part, and to erect one of the newly invented reflecting cylinders. This consisted of a cylinder of mirrors around which were fitted oil burners.

About this time the Low Light, which had been lit by candles, showed signs of decay. It stood at the bottom of Swan Score, known later as Mariner's Score. Gillingwater says that in 1735 a movable timber-frame lighthouse was built, but this was replaced by a tubular steel erection in 1867. This burnt oil and had an occult light—a light cut off for a shorter period than the period of light. There was a fog signal bell on the gallery. The Low Light was demolished about 1923.

The High Light was repaired and improved in 1825 and again in 1840, but was replaced by a new one built in 1873. This had a dioptric lantern lit by oil, but is now lit by electricity. Unlike the light at Southwold and Orford, it is manned by a keeper. Lowestoft can still boast of being the oldest Trinity House station in existence. It gives a white light, revolving every half minute and is visible for 17 miles.

The Orford Light (1637) is also occulting, of white, red and green, visible for 15 miles. Walter White, writing in 1865, asked why there was no lighthouse at Southwold. He was told: "We don't want one, there's no sand here. 'Tis a deep water bay." But they built one in 1890, a land-housed light, that is called a group occulting light of white and red sections, visible for 17 miles.

The Southwold Lighthouse

There was a light at Pakefield in 1832 and another at Land-guard, Felixstowe in 1838. This was destroyed by fire and never replaced.

The last of the seamarks—that at Bawdsey—was demolished in 1924 because of coast erosion, but church steeples were often used in this connection. There were signal stations at Felixstowe, Bawdsey, Orford, Aldeburgh, Dunwich, Easton Cliff—once the most easterly point, but washed away; Covehithe, Kessingland and Gunton. Tar barrels were placed on the church towers at Lowestoft and Woodbridge.

Other precautions were the martello towers, of which there were many along the coast, and which have become such pic-turesque pieces of our coastal scenery. They were built in 1803 on the recommendation of the Duke of York, the then Commander-in-Chief. The name is derived from Cape Mortello in Corsica, where a circular tower of this kind was captured only after great difficulty by British forces in 1794, supporting Corsican insurgents against the French revolutionaries. It was because of this stubborn defence that they were adopted in England, and seventy-four towers were erected on the most vulnerable stretches of the English Channel coast. They are 30 to 40 feet high, with walls of 9 feet thick on the seaward side, and surrounded by a ditch. Entry was gained by a small door in the rear at the head of a 20-foot ladder. A platform held two howitzers and a swivel gun. A powder magazine and living quarters were below. They lost most of their usefulness with the advent of the powerful naval guns, but were of considerable value to the Coastguard service.

The bays along the coast are shallow, that of Hollesley being protected by the Whiting sandbank. It was here that Nelson thought Napoleon would attempt a landing. The other bay is at Southwold, known as Sole Bay, the scene of the great naval battle between ourselves and the French, against the Dutch.

The Romans found it necessary to protect the coast even in their day, hence the great fort of Burgh Castle, the best preserved specimen of their work to be found in England. They also built another at Walton, or possibly a signal station, which has been swallowed by the sea and in the tergiversation of times has become Felixstowe. Between these two points, sites have been noted at Corton, Covehithe, Easton Bavents and Dunwich. There must have been some communication between these possible signal stations.

There is a natural phenomenon which has had, and continues to have, a great effect on our coastline, viz. the southward thrust of the tides. This has caused the silting up of the river mouths, such as we have seen at Aldeburgh and at Lowestoft, and the creation of the spur at Landguard Point. Its chiefly noticeable effect was at Dunwich, where the river mouth was constantly on the move until it became established at Walberswick.

Then, of course, the whole coastline has been subject to erosion, with hardly any place that has not been affected. The lost land of Suffolk has been very great, and still goes on; where the sea is kept at bay at one place by means of groynes and sea defences, it breaks in at another. One has only to mention places such as Covehithe, Pakefield, Aldeburgh and Slaughden. There has been encroachment at Corton, and a hamlet called Newton has entirely disappeared. The Low lighthouse at Lowestoft was twice moved back, and it is said the Ness was cut back 1,100 feet between 1854 and 1901, when defence works were commenced and arrested the tide.

In fact the whole of our coastline has been modified to quite an unknown degree. For example, it is thought to have extended five miles further seaward than Easton Bavents does today; while Dunwich has been given the credit of seven miles.

From Lowestoft to Aldeburgh several small streams have been dammed back by shingle. This is mentioned in the Butley Cartulary, where it is noted that the mouths of the rivers at Kessingland, Benacre, Dunwich, Minsmere and the little Hundred river at Aldeburgh were then open and several havens. Each of these is now dammed by sand and shingle.

Storms have raged with great effect, and it was said there were more total wrecks off Aldeburgh than any part of the coast, except Gorleston. The story of the Aldeburgh lifeboats, coupled with the name of Cable, is an epic in itself.

Dunwich was undoubtedly the most interesting of the old Suffolk ports. It must seem almost incredible that the cluster of houses that now form this tiny hamlet was the capital city of East Anglia, and here was the premier port on this side of England, greater by far than Ipswich or even London itself.

The rise to greatness of Dunwich lay in its shipping, and it must be realized that the fisheries were the foundation of traffic by sea and the source of much wealth. This is evident because the fee farm rent was in herrings for centuries, and a herring appears on the seal of the bailiff of the town.

Kessingland also has its tales of shipwrecks, and the melancholy fate of a shipwrecked crew is recorded in the register: "Buried November 27 1774, Adam Laurie, James Nisbet, Andrew Miller, John Laurie, his wife and four children, whose vessel being wrecked, and they having escaped from the fury of the winds and waves, and being sheltered under the cliff, were by the earth falling on them overwhelmed with a sudden and unexpected death, on the 24th., November, 1774."

The first recorded appearance of the Norsemen was in A.D. 835, and the Danes came in force in 866. In 876, however, the Danish army left Wareham, and it is conjectured that Guthrum (who is supposed to be buried in Hadleigh church) travelled by sea, embarking from Orwell Haven. The Vikings attacked the Danes in 884, and a battle was fought in 885 at the mouth of the Stour and at Shotley Point, when sixteen Danish ships were captured and the crews killed.

This is the first known sea fight directly connected with Suffolk and Essex. However, the victors were themselves defeated on their return journey by a superior force. In 980 the Danish incursions recommenced, and in 991 Ipswich was plundered.

In 1205 appeared the first station of the king's ships, when two galleys are recorded as belonging to Ipswich, but five at Dunwich. Then in 1225 the sheriffs of Norfolk and Suffolk were directed to select three ships at Ipswich, fitted for horse transport; and if they were not to be obtained there they were to be taken from Dunwich. Indeed, of all the Suffolk ports, Dunwich stands out pre-eminently as the one on which the Crown relied as always having ships and men available.

It is interesting to note that a wine trade with Gascony developed, one of the ships so engaged being of 125 tons. Orford, Ipswich and Goseford, as well as Dunwich, are referred to as passage ports, and it is of great interest to know the variety of enterprises that contributed to the commerce of those days.

For instance, in the fifteenth century there was a considerable

Fishermen's huts on the stoney beach at Aldeburgh

traffic in the passage of pilgrims to the shrine of St. James of Compostella. Many and various must have been the types that set sail from our coast. When they returned, tired and dishevelled, they would be wearing an escallop shell as a sign of accomplishment. This often figures in heraldry and on our churches. Our shipmasters must have been equal to the occasion, for this must have been the first of the packaged holidays.

Orford, Ipswich and Dunwich are specified as ports in the years 1230–55, but Gosford was grouped with Ipswich and Orwell in 1242. The State Papers for 1565 give a full list of ports, creeks and landing places of the county: the ports being Gorleston (then in Suffolk), Lowestoft, Easton, Southwold, Walberswick, Dunwich, Aldeburgh, Orford and Ipswich. A few years later the Lowestoft men objected that the place was not a port, nor a member of any port, and were for ever pleading poverty. Orwell Haven was the best harbour south of the Humber and the best victualling station, because of the fertility of the surrounding district. Commercially and militarily it has been the chief port of Suffolk.

Orford Haven was showing signs of its ultimate decay in 1584, but Hollesley Bay in the days of sail always was a favourite anchorage, for between Orfordness and Lowestoft Roads there was no shelter. Orwell Haven was a safe and roomy retreat, although sandbanks sometimes made the entrance troublesome.

Shipbuilding was carried on at various places, notably at Dunwich by the famous Kett family, who probably hailed from Harwich. At Aldeburgh it was started by the Johnson family, who eventually moved to Blackwall. Ipswich became famous for its ships, because of the plentiful supply of local timber. In fact it was known as the shipyard of London. It was also a great place for cordage and canvas. Then the first two warships of the then modern navy to be built in Suffolk came from Woodbridge— the *Advice* and the *Reserve*, both of 42 tons. They must have got safely over those pernickety bars at Bawdsey Haven. Ipswich ceased as a shipyard of any tonnage owing to the silting up of the Orwell. Although the *Henry Grace de Dieu* was not built in Suffolk yards, shipwrights and caulkers from Ipswich, Dunwich, Southwold and Lowestoft helped to build it.

Suffolk has a great heritage of the sea, its heroes are innumerable, but, like so much else of nobility, mainly unsung. It was one of their own salt who said: "Wet and cold cannot make them shrink nor strain whom the North Sea has dyed in grain."

Our coast has been always chiefly concerned in the fishing industry, especially the herring. Dunwich at one time was the chief fishing port and sent ships to Iceland fishing for cod and ling for many years. In a report made January 1565–6, regarding this industry, Dunwich was said to possess 166 mariners and one ship of 100 tons and upwards; while another list made in 1570 gives 105 mariners. The vessels used to bear strange names, such as crayers, busses, pinks and ketches; moreover, they were 'wafted' by naval vessels, otherwise they were at the mercy of the pirates that infested these waters and failed to return. As Dunwich fortunes declined so the trade shifted to Southwold, Kessingland, Lowestoft and Yarmouth.

Herrings move in shoals, emerging from the Arctic Ocean in the early summer on their southward migration. The day for commencing the herring voyage to the Shetlands was St. John's Day, and hundreds of busses from Suffolk would rendezvous there, and from thence follow the shoals up the North Sea. Herrings are caught all through the year off some parts of the British coasts, but at Lowestoft the principal season is from September to about the middle of December when the fish arrive off our coast. Lowestoft is the chief Suffolk port for this industry with its trawl fishing. This North Sea fishing has been always a dangerous occupation, and many men have lost their lives. On the north wall of the north aisle of St. Margaret's church, Lowestoft, there is a Fishermen's Memorial, listing the names of those lost at sea.

At Southwold small boats are engaged in inshore trawling for sole and plaice, while lining for cod is also done. Sprats are caught in great numbers by Southwold, Aldeburgh and Thorpe fishermen, from October to the end of January. From April to November shrimps are caught by trawling, and lobsters and crabs are a local catch along the coast. It might also be mentioned that, whereas herrings are caught by trawling, mackerel are taken by drifters.

This is a fisherman's prayer:

Pray God lead us;
Pray God speed us;
From all evil defend us.
Fish for our pains God send us.
Well to fish and well to haul,
And what He pleases to pay us all.
A fine night to land our nets,
And safe in with the haul.
Pray God hear my prayer.

For centuries it was the custom at Yarmouth and Lowestoft to pay tithe on fish to the vicars of the respective parish churches, both on the herring and mackerel fisheries. This was known as 'Christ's Half-Dole'. An attempt to revive it was made in the middle of last century, but was soon dropped.

The Suffolk coast has been the scene of comings and goings during the long centuries of our island story. In 1338, when the turbulent Edward III was at war with both France and Scotland, claiming the crown of France, fifteen ships of local tonnage were assembled at Goseford for an expedition to Flanders. These had a complement of fifteen masters, fifteen mates, 481 mariners and eleven boys. Their destination was Antwerp. Then in 1340 a fleet of some 250 ships sailed from the mouth of the Orwell to gain a decisive victory over the French fleet at Sluys. This was the first battle to establish English supremacy on the seas.

Naturally enough our coast figured in the threatened attack by the Spanish Armada of 1588, when sundry ships were commissioned to await the onslaught, such as the *Vanguard* of Harwich, *William and Catherine* of Ipswich and the *Sallowman* of Aldeburgh. An account has been recorded of Lord Henry Seymour's movements while seeking to come up with the Spanish fleet: "The 31st. day we had to wind SSW, and we reached as high as Badsey Cliff, there we were obliged to anchor in the sea, with very much wind upon the ebb, about 3 o'clock in the afternoon, and so continued all that day and the night following. The 1st of August as we were weighing anchor to windward the Lord Henry Seymour sent the pinnace called Delight and ordered us to go round to Harwich to take in our provisions. And about 1 o'clock we anchored at Harwich."

These were days of high pressure, but the Government prudently directed that the drilling of the land forces was to be suspended at harvest time to prevent scarcity of supplies and impoverishment of the farmers. All men above 16 and under 60 were required to attend muster for the purpose of being drilled.

The First Dutch War broke out in 1652, when Admiral Blake destroyed the Dutch herring fleet in the North Sea, and the Orwell was used as a naval base. Then in the following year the English sighted the Dutch off the Gabbard at Orford Ness at the beginning of the battle of the North Foreland. Blake was severely wounded and brought ashore at Walberswick, at which place he could get no succour.

In 1665, during the Second Dutch War, the Duke of York defeated the Dutch off Lowestoft and landed 2,000 prisoners, who were housed in various Suffolk towns. One of these left a memento behind when he scratched the outline of a Dutch vessel on the wall of Melton Gaol in 1681.

The only landing on Suffolk soil was made in 1666, when about 2,000 men were actually landed on Felixstowe beach. The troops stationed at Lowestoft, Southwold, Dunwich and Aldeburgh were withdrawn from thence and concentrated at Landguard. "Seven colliers, and a ship of 20 guns, all disguised as men-of-war, with Jack, Ensign and pennants, were laid across the arm of the sea, from Landguard Fort to the slide beacon, with holes cut, ready to be sunk in case of the enemy approach." The attack was made on 2nd July. The intention of the enemy was to take the fort by scaling the walls on the landward side, where it was most vulnerable. The attack was driven off by the then commander, Captain Darrell, who sustained a slight musket shot wound in the shoulder. All this for the loss of three or four men killed and as many wounded, while the attackers' losses were about 150.

The chief engagement off our coast was that of the Battle of Sole Bay in the Dutch wars; that was fought in May 1672. The fleets of Britain and France were combined against the Dutch. The former were 101 sail of men-of-war, besides fire-ships and tenders, carrying 6,018 guns and 34,500 men. The latter, including fire-ships and tenders, mustered 168, of which 91 were men-of-war. The commanders of the combined squadron were James Duke of York, Count D'Estrees and the Earl of Sandwich.

For the Dutch were De Ruyter, Blankart and Van Ghent, accompanied by Cornelius De Witt as deputy from the states.

It appears that the English and French lay in the bay in a very vulnerable position with regard to fire-ships. The Earl of Sandwich warned his brother commanders, but the Duke of York took umbrage, considering it as a reflection on his courage. When the enemy appeared there was a scramble amongst our ships to disentangle themselves, and it was Sandwich who helped in this matter. He attacked the entire squadron of Van Ghent single-handed, killing the Dutch admiral with his own hand, sinking a man-of-war and three others of the enemy vessels.

However, his own ship was grappled and fired. He fought on amid the flames, but finally jumped into the sea. Later his body was found, wearing the Star of the Garter and three diamond rings on his fingers. It was taken to Landguard Fort to be embalmed, and rested in the chapel there. He was described as a "wonderful fat man, and his heart was strangely covered with fat. There was not a pint of water run from him, but his being so mightily swelled proceeded rather from wind than water." Possibly he died of shock. He received a public funeral and was buried in Henry VII Chapel at Westminster. His Suffolk home was at Shrubland Park.

The Duke of York was hotly pressed by De Ruyter, so much so that, of the thirty-two engagements in which he had fought, he declared this to be the sharpest and longest. His own ship, the *Royal James*, was lost, and he had to change ship three times. Night brought the battle to a close, and the losses on both sides were about equal. The Dutch losses were forbidden to be published at home. It is said the French ships scarcely took any share in the action and for the most part kept out of reach of danger. A thick fog which came up suddenly hampered proceedings. In any case the Dutch fled. Naturally local poets rose to the occasion:

> One day as I was sitting still
> Upon the side of Dunwich hill,
> And looking on the ocean.
> By chance I saw De Ruyter's fleet
> With Royal James's squadron meet;
> In sooth it was a noble treat
> To see that brave commotion.

Well might you hear their guns, I guess,
From Sizewell-gap to Easton-ness,
The show was rare and sightly;
They battered without let or stay,
Until the evening of that day:
'Twas then the Dutchmen ran away—
The Duke had beat them tightly.

Landguard Fort was first built in the reign of Charles I and was completed in 1627–8. But it is pretty evident that some sort of bulwark—probably in the nature of an earthwork—existed there as early as the sixteenth century. As one stands at the old place, looking out over the parapets, one is forced to conclude that the old engineers and defenders of our realm knew what they were doing. It is a most marvellous spot of strategic importance, commanding the confluence of the waters.

The earliest reference to the importance of Langer, as it was then referred to, was on the advent of the Armada. At the time, 1587, the garrison at Harwich consisted of 17,000 men, with Plymouth having the same number and Portsmouth a thousand fewer. This speaks for itself. In a "Survey of the Coast of Suffolk, December 13, 1587", it is stated: "Touching the Fortifications of the Coast of Suffolk, Langer Poynt we fynde to be a place of as great danger as any we have in this Cowntie so apt for the enemy to lande at, as without helpe or use of boates, they may leape on land owte of their shippes." But, as all the world knows, there was no invasion of our coast by the Spaniards. Neither was there a fort at Landguard.

In 1621, however, it was realized that steps ought to be taken that all the coast be put in a state of defence, so the first fort came into existence. This was described as a "handsome square fortification, consisting of four bastions, at each corner one, mounted with divers guns, those over towards the sea being the largest, the entrance into it was over a drawbridge, through a gate, over which was their magazine; fronting the gate was a handsome brick building, in which the governor, when he was there, resided; adjoining to the south-east of which was a neat chapel, in which the chaplain said prayers twice a week, and preached a sermon on a Sunday." It might be mentioned that a drawbridge figures in all three forts, because the site was moated. There is a reference to this in 1635: "The moate is not yet finished, nor the counterscarpe whereby the fort itself is left in undefensive condition." It was from this fort, completed in 1626, that the Dutch were beaten off in 1667, after they had successfully attacked both Sheerness and Chatham.

During the Civil War, it is interesting to note that Landguard Fort was held for the Parliament. But then East Anglia in general was for the Commonwealth all through the war. Lord Fairfax visited the fort after the siege of Colchester, and Colonel Thomas Ireton, brother to the General Ireton, was a governor at the time. The sort of ammunition then used is of interest: "Barrells of powder 92, Demy Cannon round shott 200, Culverin round shott 380, Demy Culverin round shott 270, Saken round shott 270, Crossbar shott of all sorts, about 250. Match about three quarters of a tun."

It was on 28th May 1672 that the body of the Earl of Sandwich, Admiral of the Blue, was brought to the fort and embalmed by order of Sir Charles Lyttleton, who wrote on 4th June: "he lyes in my chappell in his coffin, with black bays over it, and some black bays and scutcheons round the chappell, which is all the ceremony this place will afford, till further directions. When ye body was gone of in ye boate we fired some volleys of small shot, and after 21 great guns from ye Fort. I thought it undecent to part without some such, because its being here was so publicly known, though they have order to passe through the Fleet with all privacy."

It would appear that the old fort of 1626 provided a continuous case for a moan. The place was falling to pieces, the food was awful, the pay was shocking.

In October 1708 orders were given by the council to the officers of the Ordnance to lay before Parliament an estimate "for enlarging the fortifications at Landguard Fort and fortifying Harwich". The sum involved was £10,801, but was subsequently reduced in amount. Nothing, however, was done about this. In 1715 its condition was once again brought to the notice of the Surveyor General of Ordnance: "I take leave once again to remind you of a representation from the Board relating to Landguard Fort, which is in so bad a condition, that neither the Fort, Barraques, or Storehouses can be repaired, and it is proposed to bring to Harwich, the people and stores and lodge them where the King has Houses until the Fort can be rebuilt, which will take up some time to provide the materials of, particularly the Bricks must be contracted for in the neighbourhood—the winter season drawing near I hope will be an excuse for this trouble."

This is of great interest, particularly the reference to the bricks, which must have been made locally. Those massive old walls still remain a ponderous memorial to old time brick-makers and bricklayers. So the new fort of 1716 came into existence, and was completed in 1720. It was this fort which the youthful Gainsborough sketched for one of the governors. Although it was a fine and imposing structure for the time, its armaments were greatly reduced; formerly mounting sixty-three guns, it was now allotted but twenty.

The inception of the new fort, and the subsequent reduction in armaments, resulted in a certain loss of dignity. Forts were divided into three classes: forts where the Union Jack is flown on anniversaries only, or when specially required for saluting purposes; where the flag is flown on Sundays and anniversaries; where it is flown daily. However, Landguard soon not only recovered any lost rights but also became one of the flag stations at which the Royal Standard could be flown on Royal anniversaries and State occasions. It was also one of the 230 saluting stations in Great Britain; but it must be realized that the flagstaff was Navy.

The fort of 1716 came to an end; in 1871 the War Office decided that it should be entirely reconstructed and rearmed. This was done and completed in 1875. All the old buildings were pulled down, but the new fort was built inside the old one.

In this 1875 fort the old order meets the new, and it is a most fascinating study. It must be recalled that in those days of Victoria, the guns were muzzle loaders, and the elevating tackle still remains at the portholes, with iron swivel brackets, spiralled to take the ropes. This takes us back to the days of Nelson and the wooden walls of England. Then it must be recalled lighting was of the most primitive kind, therefore it is not surprising to discover that the subterranean corridors leading to the ammunition chambers have embrasures where tallow candles were placed. One wonders if they made their own candles, with tallow imported from

Russia. The last pre-electric lamps were for oil and were made by Sherwoods Ltd. of Birmingham; some are still in existence.

Throughout its long history there seems to have been four bastions. They still exist in name, known as the Right Battery, Beacon Hill Battery, Darell's Battery and Angel Battery. Why the latter I cannot say, unless it was deemed the quickest way to Heaven. It is also of great interest to note that visional shooting prevailed until within three months of the end of the 1939–45 war. It then became radar controlled.

Major Leslie, who wrote the history of the fort, says: "The records of Landguard Fort are justly worthy of a place amongst the traditions of Great Britain and her defenders."

In the *Illustrated London News* for 1888 there appeared a series of articles with pictures of our coastal defences. Naturally Landguard figures in these, wherein the old cry of 1621 is raised again. The theme of the reprint was all too familiar. It states that the Medway entering the Thames inlet at Sheerness was of considerable importance to the military defence of London, particularly as it contained Chatham. It maintained that the coast from Southend to Colchester was very vulnerable. Farther on, the port of Harwich, described as the North Sea port of London, gave access to a large tract of country comparatively destitute of military defences. All this concerned more or less the safety of the metropolis, which could be assailed from the east by a hostile army with fewer obstacles in view of the natural features of the country than from the Sussex coast.

Then comes this, so characteristic of our character: "It might be indiscreet to give particulars of the numbers and efficiency of the guns at present mounted on our fortifications; and we can never be sure that some of them, *such as they are* [my italics], may not be taken away to put on board some ship of the Royal Navy which is unprovided with guns needed for her own service while making them continuously for foreign nations."

Now follows a description of Harwich, concluding with: "The harbour entrance is commanded by Landguard Fort, on a spit of sand projecting from the Suffolk coast opposite Harwich, and by the Angel Gate battery and the redoubt near Beacon Hill, adjacent to this Esplanade. We have noted among the recommendations of the War Office Committee, that the needful defences of Harwich are in the mind of the Government, and we trust they will not be neglected."

It is a curious fact that in the short period under review two German emperors died and were buried in all the pomp and circumstance of deep mourning. A young man then ascended the throne, and his wife and young children were to pay a visit to Felixstowe on holiday bent. It was his Germany that was destined to wage the continental war that our fathers feared might come. Although I think I am right in saying that those guns of Landguard never fired an angry shot. Time plays strange tricks, and is often best seen in retrospect. Now, owing to the vicissitudes of war and its powers of destruction, the old fort has been abandoned and the flag dismantled. Perchance it may come to life again as a museum.

We might end this chapter with a verse or two of *Sea-Side Flowers* by Agnes Strickland, recalling that the area around the old fort is a good hunting ground for rare specimens:

> The wild sea cliff, though rude it be,
> Is wreathed with many a flower,
> That blossoms there, unscathed and free,
> Through storms and shower.

Amongst the many verses she mentions the horned poppy, stone crop, redbind, burnet, eringo, borrage, grey lichens, persicaria, samphire, wormwood, behen, bugloss and chrysanthemum.

> Tis sweet, in pleasant hours like these,
> To pace the glittering sand,
> And court the light caressing breeze
> That sweeps the strand.
>
> And whirl the blow-balls' new-fledged pride
> In mossy rings on high,
> Whose downy pinions, once untied,
> Must onwards fly.

4

Brandon
and the Flint Knappers

There was no market-town in all
The land of the Iceni
Where Johnny did not loudly call
For ev'rybody's guinea.

Cowper

East Anglia possesses two tracts of land the like of which can be found nowhere else in England. One is the primeval forest of Staverton, near Butley, the other is Breckland, half of which is in Suffolk and the other in Norfolk. In the centre of this most unusual country is the little town of Brandon, forming as it were an outpost of the county and an outpost of an ancient civilization. Here is a peculiar scenery dominated by twisted pine trees, flints in cottage walls and buildings of all kinds. It is indeed a land steeped in the past. After all there is nothing like a wind-blown tree to create a sense of desolation and awesomeness. A few years ago, when W. G. Clarke wrote his book and gave the name of Breckland to the vast areas of brecks, it was a land of wide spaces and a scene of forbidding loneliness, with a shifting soil of sand and loose flinty pebbles, where stone-curlews laid their two eggs in a hollow scraped in the sand. Now, owing to the work of the Forestry Commission and since the first state forest was planted in 1922, the open heathland has greatly diminished, so that even W. G. Clarke, who knew every inch of the area (so much so that he knew every species of birds and plants in a given part), would not be able to recognize it. He died in 1925.

The villages of Lakenheath, Lackford, Eriswell, Flempton and the two Icklinghams; and the towns of Mildenhall, Brandon and Thetford, all partake of this rather strange, almost eerie character that broods over such a flint-dominated landscape. Mildenhall and Lakenheath have almost become outposts of American military aviation, but Thetford Chase with its 48,000 acres, reminds us

A flint knapper's cottage, Brandon

of the once treeless tracts to be found hereabouts—now covered with alien conifers.

The Breckland villages might be mentioned in brief. Wordwell has a little Norman church with sculptured tympana to its north and south doorways. Lackford has a late thirteenth-century font of very fine design. Eriswell church has a wall-painting of the Miraculous Draught of Fishes, which was a subject never used by the old painters. Lakenheath church tower is curiously placed rather east of the west end. It was at Lakenheath that Sir John Cavendish was slain; and it was at Lakenheath that Charles Wesley preached the first ever Methodist sermon in Breckland in 1754. Mildenhall is the most extensive parish in Suffolk, of nearly 17,000 acres, half of which was anciently fen. It includes a number of hamlets such as Beck Row, West Row, Kenny Hill. The church is spacious and very fine, while nearby in the old manor house lived Sir Thomas Hanmer, Speaker and Shakespearean critic.

The late Claude Morley said this: "Brandon may be considered the centre of the Breck district, one of those most interesting tracts of heathland to the archaist and naturalist in Britain. In this sense 'Breck' is a quite local word unknown outside East Anglia, with the meaning of ground that has been broken up by tilth; I expect during Knut's time, about 1020."

There were also the two great stretches known as Thetford Warren and Wangford Warren, covered with a minute and lichen-like vegetation and crowned with a fern-like brake. This was the haunt of game and was guarded by an army of warreners. They wore a long blouse or slop which reached below the knees, and seemed to be a race apart. Their headquarters was Warren Lodge, situated in the middle of this lonely area. These warreners were also skilled gamekeepers.

This may well have been the reason why the Maharajah Duleep Singh purchased Elveden Hall in 1863, and turned this lonely oasis into a miniature India. After all, he was much given to sport, particularly shooting. In a recent book entitled *The Maharajah*, it is stated that the young Sikh prince used to refer in private to Queen Victoria as "Mrs. Fagin . . . a receiver of stolen property", because she had taken from him the Koh-i-noor diamond. But he had accepted a large pension, made her god-mother to his son and lived the life of an English gentleman in East

Anglia. Also he spent a great deal of time at the English court. Although he spent a long time in Paris, he is buried in the church-yard at Elveden.

Eventually the property was bought by the first Lord Iveagh, who turned to farming and created the largest farm in all England—a tribute to modern farming methods and the reclamation of waste land.

It is not without significance that Breckland produced one of Suffolk's best known poets—Robert Bloomfield, author of *The Farmer's Boy*. Out from that rather arid scenery came this delightful little volume, which has never lost its fragrance or its appeal. Perhaps it is explained by the one-time belief in fairies attributed to those descendants of Neolithic tribes, who were a peace-loving people. And the folk-lore gave birth to the White Rabbit said to haunt the warrens near Thetford. It had large flaming eyes that portended disaster, and was so fleet of foot that it could never be caught. Fairies, indeed, found a lodgement in much of Suffolk. And yet it was said that few of the Breckland cottages possessed a garden.

Brandon is on the Little Ouse, which was navigable as far as Lynn in one direction and Thetford in the other. Between the Town Bridge at Thetford and Brandon Bridge are nearly 9 miles, a district that was so well known to the poet.

For centuries Brandon possessed a picturesque seventeenth-century bridge that consisted of four irregular arches, which after so many long years of traffic and navigation was considered unsafe. Under the signature Frederick Duleep Singh (who was the son of the Maharajah of Elveden, otherwise known as the Black Prince) this letter appeared in *Country Life* for 5th November 1910.

The object of my letter is to appeal to you to allow the voice of Country Life to be raised in trying to save another old bridge that is threatened, and one that, being on a little known river, would otherwise escape notice of the general public. I refer to the bridge over the Little Ouse at Brandon. This river used formerly to be the boundary between the counties of Norfolk and West Suffolk, but owing to an agreement between the respective County Councils, the whole of the town of Brandon is now included in Suffolk, so that it is the Council of the latter County that has sole control of the

matter. I understand that the County Council has been advised that the bridge is absolutely unsafe and must be rebuilt; and I am informed privately, by members of the Council, that there is very little likelihood of the old bridge being retained, and no doubt a cast-iron monstrosity, such as has been erected by the County Councils of Norfolk and West Suffolk at Lakenheath, will take its place. This would be a great calamity, as Brandon Bridge is one of the oldest and most picturesque in the Eastern Counties.

Evidently this plea saved the old bridge for many years, because a new one was not erected until after years of cavilling, in 1952–3, when the exigencies of modern traffic demanded a new one. This is simply designed, faced with knapped flints as becomes such an area. However, if a cast-iron monstrosity had been erected, it would have found great favour in these days, although it too would have gone the way of all things.

Navigation on this rather swiftly-flowing stream was made possible by staunches instead of locks. There were thirty-two of these on various streams in England and seven on the Little Ouse. They had a door of oak to hold up the water. This was raised by chains working on an axle, at the end of which was a large wheel. There was a considerable traffic in corn, seeds, malt, coal, timber, iron, bricks, tiles and such like.

Lighters used to ply on this river, named after their owners. The typical fen lighter was about 42 feet long, 9 feet wide at bottom and 10 feet at deck. Their loading capacity was about 25 tons. They navigated in gangs of about five, the stempost of one being coupled with the stempost of the next. A man standing on the first navigated the gang by a steering pole. They were drawn, as you might well imagine, by those lovely docile Suffolk horses that walked along the haling path, which in parts was extremely beautiful—a soft beauty of willows, reeds and marsh-milk parsley, best realized by its name of Spring Walk. This, with red roofs, flint walls and a Suffolk sky, create a picture of tranquillity reflected in the placid stream.

> It were a most delightful thing
> To live in a perpetual Spring.

Moreover, Brandon has a Victorian railway station. In the early days, at the Station Hotel nearby, the corn market was held.

The Market House, Mildenhall

The church has been much restored, but there is the lower part of a rood screen and some bench ends. One of Brandon's sons, Simon Eyre, became Lord Mayor of London! He was the builder of Leadenhall Market, over the portal of which, in Latin, was inscribed: "The right hand of the Lord hath exalted me." He was also the hero of the Shoemakers' Holiday, which I think was St. Monday.

It was said that the natives of Brandon could always be known by their brilliantly-coloured attire. This may have been a foil to the dullness of the flint houses of which the town was built. A native of Thetford, on the other hand, always walked in the middle of the road, because the paths were made of cobblestones.

Brandon was famed for what was always called Britain's oldest craft, that of flaking and knapping of flints, an industry said to derive from Palaeolithic or Neolithic times.

It has been pointed out that these early people were expert miners, because in digging down through the sand and boulder clay they were careful to leave an adequate slope to the sides to prevent slipping; but when the solid rock was reached they proceeded to drive vertical sides. Having reached the layer of flint required the miners proceeded to drive lateral galleries from the bottom main shaft and thus follow up and remove the flint seam. The pits were about 30 feet deep and over 100 prehistoric mines have been found. The earliest workings have revealed red deer antlers, with which the aboriginal miners hewed their flints, and the present-day one-sided picks differ not very materially in pattern, save that wood and iron have replaced horn.

The old flint-workings have been carried on much in the same manner as those for precious metals. Claims were staked out by means of four large pieces of chalk placed as markers at the corners, or sods of turf were dug out as boundary marks. Then the shafts were sunk, but the method of sinking differed from all other mining. Four layers or 'seases' of flints were to be found, known respectively as 'top stone', 'wall stone', 'upper crust' and 'floorstone', while flint lying in the water at the bottom of the pit was the 'blackstone'. The shafts were lighted by candles fixed in pieces of chalk. The flints were brought to the surface in buckets, which were small enough to be carried on the head.

The shaft went down 5 or 6 feet, then turned inward, right or left, for half that distance, then down again, and so on 'on the sosh' (diagonally) as the local parlance had it—until the flint layer was reached. This stage-like descent served two ends: it allowed the miner to work in safety from falling stones and also provided him with platforms at convenient heights, to which he could raise his stones until they reached the top. When about a ton had been so raised, it was called a 'jag', and was covered over with loose branches of fir to prevent the sun changing the colour of the flint and thus cheapening its value. The stone was then carted to the knapper's workshop.

The actual working involved three processes. The worker took a lump, as much as he could lift, the large nobbly pieces were trimmed off, and the remaining block quartered. Considerable force was needed to hammer off the projecting pieces, and still more skill to know just where to strike so as to leave the necessary square edges from which to produce even flakes. This was done by placing the lump on a thick leather pad on the workman's knee and striking it with a heavy-headed hammer. These hammers were hexagonal in section, weighing from $3\frac{1}{2}$ to 6 pounds, with a large face; they derive from the round pebble implements used by the ancients.

The next process was flaking, done with the same hammer, which required considerable skill. The stone had to be struck in the exact spot, at the correct angle, with a certain force that varied with each stone. The outer flakes which showed any of the white coating were waste, but when they had been struck off it was possible to produce with every stroke of the hammer a perfectly even flake about four inches long and an inch wide with a sharp edge that would cut like a knife. As the blows were struck with only a few seconds between each, it may be imagined that the skill, inherited from long years of use, was of a very high order.

Next came knapping, which was done at great speed and with fine precision. The hammer used for this process was distinctly reminiscent of the red deer antlers. It possessed a chisel-like head and was often fashioned from a flat file. The knee-pad was replaced by a large block of wood, into which a six-inch tapering iron strike was driven, padded at the sides with leather; the object was to provide the hammer-blow with a rebound. The flake was held face uppermost on the stake, and the operation knapped off fragments, each flake making four or five flints. The most skilful knapper could turn out up to 400 finished gun flints in an hour.

Wars have materially affected Brandon. In Napoleonic times they worked overtime to provide the old flint-locks with fire power. They were also busy in the days of the Crimea, working for the Turkish army; even in the ill-famed war between Italy and Abyssinia. The South African war called forth strike-a-lights in large numbers, because the climate made the use of matches uncertain. It is curious to reflect that in the age of our great-grandparents flints were used as an essential part of the old tinder-boxes, man's earliest method of kindling a spark for the fire or a light. Matches did not come in until the early part of Queen Victoria's reign.

The craft is picturesquely commemorated in the inn sign of the once Eagle Tavern, now renamed the 'Flint Knappers' Arms' at the corner of Thetford Road and High Street. This portrays a follower of the craft at work, and the design is appropriately set within a border of flush-work. A generation ago it was nothing uncommon to see the heap of glistening shalings in the yards where the work was done. The only modern touch of this age-old craft was the dust extractors against which the knapper sat. This was a guard against silicosis, the earliest known instance of an industrial disease. According to one report, the old knappers had the oldest known system of enumeration in all Britain. Their only numerals were one and seven, the latter, it is thought, because it is shaped like a pick. Other forms reflect Celtic influences, such as HHH for five, similar to that used by the old shepherds in telling sheep.

Following flint knapping, pottery at Wattisfield has been going on since the dawn of history, because of the local earth.

An old street in Bury St. Edmunds

South chapel of Lavenham church built in 1525 in commemoration of the richest commoner in England, Thomas Spring III

Hadleigh Deanery Tower built in 1495 by Archdeacon Pykenham and painted by Gainsborough. The extension to the right is Victorian

Bury St. Edmunds: abbey ruins with the cathedral in the background

Kersey Mill

Wickham Market Mill

Near Hadleigh – once a hop-growing area

The outskirts of Stowmarket

The eleventh–century, thatched chancel of St. Edmund's Church at Fritton. A Suffolk village for a millennium, Fritton was transferred to Norfolk in 1974

River Deben near Ufford

5

Suffolk Churches

For night's swift dragons cut the clouds full fast
And yonder shines Aurora's harbinger;
At whose approach, ghosts, wandering here and there,
Troop home to churchyards.

A Midsummer Night's Dream

Before considering the Suffolk church as a building, it is necessary to note something of the origin of Christianity in the county.
This was first introduced in or about 630–36 by St. Felix, who
came at the invitation of Siegebert to Dunwich, where he set up
his see. According to Bede:

> At Donmock than was Felix first Bishop,
> Of Eastangle and taught the chrysten Faith
> That is full hye in Heaven I hope.

Felix was a Burgundian missionary monk whom the young
king had met in Gaul. He is described by Bede as being full of
burning zeal to evangelize dark places of Britain. Bede continued:

Whose good endeavours herein the Bishop Felix fathered to his
great glory, and when Felix came from the coasts of Burgundy
(where he was born and took holy orders) to Honorius the Archbishop and had opened his longing unto him, the Archbishop sent
him to preach the word of life to the aforesaid natives of the East
English. Where certain his desires fell not in vain; nay rather this
good husbandman of the spiritual soil found in that nation manifest
fruit of people that believed.

For according to the good abodement of his name he brought all
that province now delivered from their long iniquity and unhap-
piness, unto faith and works of justice and the gifts of unending
happiness; and he received the see of his bishopric in the City of
Donmoc; where when he had ruled the same province seventeen
years in that dignity, he ended his life in peace in that same place.

He was succeeded by Thomas, his deacon, then by Boniface who had several aliases, and finally by Bisus or Bosa, who in 669 divided the diocese into two, continuing one at Dunwich, whose jurisdiction was within Suffolk, and the other at North Elmham, to deal with Norfolk. This last has been always open to argument as to whether the Suffolk or Norfolk Elmham was the place. So that you get this sort of thing: "In both cases the foundation of a church is traced back by experts to the end of the seventh century. In both cases it was built in the midst of an enclosure of older date. In both cases there was an episcopal residence, rebuilt at South Elmham St. Margaret by Bishop Herbert de Losinga, and embattled at North Elmham by Bishop de Spencer. In both cases the episcopal property existed before and after the Conquest."

It would appear that many parish churches were built during the two centuries these early Christians proclaimed the faith. The Danish invasion of 866 extinguished both bishoprics and apparently laid waste to every monastery and parish church in the two counties. Of Dunwich no more is heard, but Elmham was re-established about 960, and at the same time there was a tremendous activity in rebuilding the parish churches and some of the abbeys.

At Eye a labourer dug up a bronze seal in his garden, and noticing it as something of a novelty he gave it to one of his children to play with. The child, tiring of the new toy, threw it into the fire, but happily it was rescued by the mother. It proved to be a seal-die, mitre-shaped, consisting of a tier of nine wolves' heads, originally with garnets for eyes, one of which remains. The inscription on the seal suggests it belonged to Ethelwald, Bishop of Dunwich (845–70).

Yet another remarkable find was made in 1972 by a Mr. Arthur Davey of Rattlesden, whilst hoeing on a piece of land. It was a gilt bronze statuette of St. John the Evangelist, $3\frac{3}{4}$ inches high, depicting a rather youthful saint holding his right hand to his face apparently in deep thought. His gospel is propped up in a fold of his garment above his left hand. It dates from the twelfth century and realized the remarkable price of 35,000 guineas★ at Christie's. Like the bronze seal found at Eye, its discovery led to an adven-

★ 35,000 guineas is £36,750.

Hemley Church with its brick tower

ture, because Mr. Davey gave it to his son aged 7 to play with. Boylike he was willing to swop it for a friend's toy car. But the friends had only a toy tractor, so the exchange did not take place.

Mildenhall has been denominated as Clovesho, where annual councils were supposed to take place in 673. And a writer in the *Proceedings of the Suffolk Institute of Archaeology* for 1922 has claimed, rather convincingly, that St. Botolph, the pioneer of the Benedictine rule in England, built his monastery in 654 at Ikanhoe, which he identifies as Iken on the bend of the Ore or Alde. This was destroyed in 870.

By Domesday well over 300 churches are shown in both Norfolk and Suffolk. The Normans were great builders, and their style of architecture is well known, because so much of their work remains in doorways and windows. The churches, with the priories, were staffed by local men as the preponderance of East Anglian place-names as patronymics would suggest.

Beyond that fact, they must have inherited a good many churches of Saxon origin, because, according to the late Claude Morley, the long and short quoins are traceable in more than 140 of our present churches and are best represented in Debenham tower. Moreover, the Fritton apse, with its groined roof and splay of east Saxon windows, is a shining example. Then Stowlangtoft and St. Lawrence Ilketshall are on the site of Roman camps.

The Black Death killed many masons, and new ones had to be trained. It was at its worst in 1349. Two thousand clergy died in the Norwich diocese and 800 parishes lost their incumbents. However, a local immigration in the fourteenth century of Flemish weavers had an important effect for some of our imposing village churches came into being out of the profits of that trade. This has perplexed many people, who cannot understand why small villages of less than 200 inhabitants needed such cathedral-like structures, built to hold 1,000. A decrease in population since those days is not the answer. This was how the Perpendicular style, which began in the West in the fourteenth century, came into Suffolk. We are told that the finest of all fifteenth-century churches are in Norfolk and Suffolk, and this is the time when the great majority of our churches were rebuilt.

Suffolk churches have been described as restrained in outline, because stone was scarce and not to be wasted. Those rubble walls, centuries old, stand not merely as the centre of village life but also as monuments of the soil from which they were digged, with here and there a bit of septaria and here and there a bit of coralline crag. The most beautiful characteristic is the use of flint flush-work, using the knapped smooth surface to adorn the bases of towers, porches and walls. The towers are battlemented, with small pinnacles at the angles, but there are few spires.

One of the most interesting examples of flush-work is to be seen in the Gipping Chapel of St. Nicholas. On the exterior walls are to be found a wonderful collection of heraldic devices, rebuses, monograms, decorated panels and other elaborate details in stone that make a study of this building one of more than usual interest. It dates from 1483.

No church in the county can be compared with Lavenham, with a nave of such fine proportions of six bays. Long Melford, recently restored, runs it close with ten bays. Blythburgh is another, rather more decayed than the other two, but a monument of art to be found in a country village. Eye (1460–84) has a noble tower, with vertical panels of flint and stone; to say nothing of its south porch. Denston (c. 1475) was a chantry college of priests; while Dennington possesses those beautiful parclose screens that fill the arches between the chancel and the chapels. Framlingham (late fifteenth century) has a tower built of flint interspersed with random blocks of white stone that sparkle in strong sunlight. It stands 96 feet high with flushwork-panelled base and plain-panelled angle buttresses. In the chancel, rebuilt about 1554 to house the Howard tombs, is one of the finest sixteenth-century Renaissance monuments in England, erected to Thomas Howard, third Duke of Norfolk.

At the little church of Syleham, where the Saxon long and short work can be seen, the south porch may have been built by Alice de la Pole, Duchess of Suffolk. It bears the arms of her parents and her husband. Then the fifteenth-century church of Hessett shows knapped flints in its south porch, with a random sprinkling of stone.

The contract for the erection of the tower of St. Andrew's church at Walberswick has survived, dating from about 1426:

This Bill indented witnesseth, that on the Tuesday next after the Feast of St. Matthew Apostle; the fourteenth year of King Henry the sixth, a Covenant was made between Thomas Bagot, Thomas Wolfard, William Ambrynghale, and Thomas Pellyng of this town of Walberswick, on the one part; and Richard Russel of Dunwich, and Adam Powle of Blythburgh, masons, on the other part, that is to say. That the aforesaid Richard and Adam shall make, or do make a steeple joined to the church of Walberswick aforesaid; with four buttresses, and one vice [staircase], and twelve foot wide and six foot thick; the walls, the walling, the tabling, and the orbing suitably, after the steeple of Tunstall, well and trewly, and competently; a door in the west also good, as the door in the steeple of Halesworth. The aforesaid Richard and Adam shall work, or do work, on the steeple aforesaid, two terms in the year, save the first year yearly, in the time of working, of setting and laying, that is to . say, between the feasts of the Annunciation of Our Lady, and St. Michael, Archangel. But if it be other manner consented on both parties, and the aforesaid Thomas Bagot, Thomas, William and Thomas, shall find all manner of material to the steeple aforesaid; that is to say, freestone, lime and calyan wat, and sand; and all manner of things that needeth to staging, and winding and schouellis [shovelling], and all manner vessels that is needful to the steeple aforesaid. And an house to work in, to eat, and drink, and to ligge [lie] in, and to make meat in; and that be had by the place of working. The aforesaid Richard and Adam shall take to the aforesaid Thomas Bagot, Thomas, William and Thomas, for the year working, 40 shillings of lawful Money of England. And a cade of full herrings each year, in time of working. And each of them a gown of lenores ones in the time of working; so that they should be good men and true to the work appointed.

This was the era when the glorious roofs were built, sometimes flat with the beams and king posts, or the marvellous hammer beams, with outstretched angels, all of which would have been coloured; and in some cases a canopy of honour provided over the holy table.

Francis Bond in his *English Church Architecture* says: "In Suffolk especially noble examples of every type abound. Nowhere in England, or indeed in Europe, are to be seen such numerous examples of scientific and artistic carpentering as in the churches of Suffolk." Munro Cautley says: "It is amazing to find no trace of iron bolts, straps or nails. The most elaborate structures rely on framing alone, the various parts being merely mortised and tenoned together and fixed with wooden pins."

Then old seating with fine benches and bench-ends adorned the nave, and perchance the aisles, although much of this was lost in numerous restorations. At Fressingfield there is a pew on the back of which can be seen all the emblems of the Passion, from the cock crowing to the seamless cloak and the dice box for casting lots as to whose it should be; and on one of the bench-ends is St. Dorothea with her basket of roses or apples. Perchance this denoted a maidens' bench. And at Ufford is the finest font cover in the whole of the country, dating from the fourteenth century. This tapers up tier on tier to the roof, from which it is suspended by a Pelican in her Piety. By a miracle this escaped the attention of the iconoclast Dowsing in his travels. It might be mentioned that the old font covers were kept locked, lest the water should be taken for medical or magical purposes. It was changed at Easter and Whitsun.

Suffolk churches are also noted for their screen work, which was a special branch of woodwork, since it has been established that the bench carver did not make screens, neither was the latter dependent on the blacksmith for elaborate decorations. It would appear that their screens, at least those of the figures of saints and fathers, were the product of different schools.

W. W. Lillie in his *Screenwork in the County of Suffolk* has this:

It is a well known axiom of the art that painting appears when architecture has reached its climax. The framed and ordered decoration of the rood screen and loft, as distinguished from the childish exuberance of the wall-painting, calls us more clearly than anything else to behold the last phase of Gothic building. For the progress of mediaeval architecture was not cut short by the Reformation, or even by the Renaissance, but was prevented by its own achievement of ripeness and perfection. It was colour, and the polyphonic music to which it bears a striking likeness, which the Protestants destroyed. This colour, therefore, once so characteristic a feature of our Suffolk churches, focuses the attention upon the whole complex achievement of fifteenth-century art.

Lillie goes on to say that during the Middle Ages colour was employed more or less strictly according to the rules of heraldry.

"Nevertheless, the standards of life were then still measured with the eye of the husbandman, and commerce itself was close to nature. It is in that land where the yellow corn stands thick and gleaming under the ocean sun, where the field-flowers spread their enamelled eyes among the rich green pastures of the broadlands that we find the characteristic work of the East Anglian school of craftsmen."

The loveliest of the Suffolk screens is at Bramfield. This is almost complete, except that two figures are missing; and there are charming little figures of angels representing the heavenly host in the blue panels of the vaulting.

Red, green, blue and gold riot in these screens, and the fragments that remain. Some of the saints and fathers stand on fields of grass or amid small plants and flowers; while others are on floors of square tiles. Their cloaks are often gorgeous, and we are apt to meet all sorts of queer members of the heavenly host that we have never heard of before, such as St. Sitha at Belstead who was the patroness of housewives and servants. She is clad in a green kirtle with scarlet cloak and tippet, bears a bunch of keys on a heavy ring or cord in one hand and points to a book with the other. Upon her head is a veil and wimple. Beneath the black edging of her skirt appear the square toes of her shoes.

Coddenham in all probability possesses the very last phase of East Anglian screen painting, for it is dated 1534 when the spoliation of the monasteries had begun.

Although Suffolk does not contain so many examples of memorial brasses as Norfolk, it has a goodly array covering a wide field. Unfortunately it suffered greatly at the hands of metal thieves and collectors. This was the sort of thing that caused Munro Cautley to rise in his wrath. Writing of Kettleburgh on the Deben he says: "In the sanctuary is the Pennington brass, 1593, with effigies of the man and his two wives. A portion of this brass was in the church chest; but in 1934 I searched for it in vain and I suppose some vile sacrilegious pilferer has acquired it." However, roughly speaking, there are some 203 brasses with effigies and about 230 inscriptions. They are a most interesting study of periods and costumes.

First come the military figures, ranging from that of Sir Robert de Bures at Acton, 1302, to that of Sir Henry Warner of Milden-

Woolpit Church

hall, 1617. Some of these are clean-shaven, others have moustaches, while John Knyvet of Mendlesham has a beard, which is an unusual feature. Needless to say, armour in all its variations and developments can be found, from chain-mail to plate.

Ecclesiastics are poorly represented. The first example is (or was) to be found at Brundish of Esmond de Burnedissh, *c.* 1360; coming down to Thomas Reve D.D., 1595, at Monewden. He was "one of ye seniorer fellows of Gunville and Cajus Colidge, Cambridge". There are also several post-Reformation divines.

There is only one judicial brass, that of John Staverton, Baron of the Exchequer, *c.* 1430, at Eyke. Also only one strictly legal gentleman, Robert Southwell, 1514, at Barham, who is styled "*apprenticus ad leges*". Also two notaries—both in the church of St. Mary Tower, Ipswich—who have ink-horn and pencase attached to their girdles.

Civilians range from John Bowf, *c.* 1417, at Pakefield, who has short hair and is wearing a long tunic with close-fitting sleeves, to Robert Alefounder, gentleman, at East Bergholt, 1639. He is wearing the costume of Charles I and appears in a doublet and cloak with riding breeches in the place of the trunk hose, with top boots, spurs and large stirrup guards.

Ladies, singly, number about forty. The earliest is Ele Bowet, 1400, in reticulated head-dress wearing a long gown buttoned down the front. The horned head-dress and close-fitting gown appears first at Yoxford, in the brass of Maud Norwich, 1428. A butterfly head-dress appears on Anne Playters, 1479, at Sotterley. Some of these ladies wear very beautiful girdles and pouches. Examples of the costumes worn during the reigns of Elizabeth and James I are at Easton.

This brings us to children, of which there are six examples. These range from a youth at Brundish, *c.* 1570, to Anne Tyrell, 1638, aged 8½ years, at Stowmarket; and include a small figure of John Shorlond, 1601, aged 7, in a doublet and petticoat.

There are six palimpsests, three of which are portions of Flemish brasses.

An interesting little touch can be found in Dennington church, in one of the box-pews next to the north wall, which was evidently appropriated by the servants at Dennington Hall. To enliven the tedium of a long sermon, this scratching appears:

Louisa Selfe is my name,
England is my nation,
Dennington is my dwelling place,
And cooking my occupation.

This is followed in like manner by the nurse, Georgiana Donald-
son, and the housemaid, Hannah Hart. In the belfry is thought
to be the oldest clock in Suffolk still going.

Buxhall church has an east window of fourteenth-century glass,
so beautiful as to have got into the *Glossary of Architecture*, according to M. R. James. A curious grant was made to a local resident
by Henry VIII, graciously allowing Walter Coppinger to wear
his cap "in our presence", because his head was so diseased "that
without his great danger he cannot be discovered of the same".

Munro Cautley reports two interesting achievements of royal
arms. One is at Rushbrooke of Henry VIII.* He remarks: "I know
of no others of this early date in the country, whilst those of
Elizabeth at Preston must be unique as an heraldic composition."

The bells in the bellcage at East Bergholt are unique in
England and are believed to be unique in Europe. What distin-
guishes them is that they are rung by being man-handled by the
ringers, whereas normal bells are rung with ropes.

Suffolk, with Norfolk, has been always noted for its church
bells, an art of early music which, alas, has fallen on bad times,
although there is more method ringing in Suffolk today than
ever. The earliest bell is that on the clock at Hadleigh, which is
inscribed, "Hail Mary full of Grace", and dates from the end of the
thirteenth century. The next was the tenor at Worlington,
inscribed, "*Johannes Godynge de Lenne me fecit*". This dates from
about the fourteenth century. It is of great interest in that the old
hythe, or staithe, could be traced in late Victorian times—
evidence that the bell might have been brought thither by water,
showing that the Lark was navigable some seven centuries ago.

The oldest of the London bells is at Barnadiston, inscribed,
"O all ye Saints of God pray for us", which Raven says may go
back to the Suffolk founders, such as William de Suffolk, potter,

---

* It is possible that the arms of Henry VIII at Rushbrooke, despite being
accurate, are an elaborate fake, created by Colonel Rushbrooke, the restorer of
the church in the nineteenth century.

1276; Philip de Ufford, potter, and Alan de Suffolk, potter. The founders' parish, by the way, was St. Botolph's without Aldgate.

The bells of the famous Brasyers' of Norwich swarm all over the county, from Bradwell to Stanningfield, from Icklingham to Wherstead. They are as remarkable for beauty as for number, according to Raven.

There was a medieval foundry at Bury St. Edmunds, which, according to the shield on their work, also produced cannon; but the fact remains that no name can be traced. Raven speculates that possibly they made guns for ships to repel the Armada. Who knows?

Miles Graye of Colchester, whom Raven describes as a prince among workmen, produced some eighty bells for Suffolk between 1605 and 1646. It would appear that the foundry was removed to Sudbury about 1686. Henry Pleasant carried on until 1707. One of his bells at St. Nicholas, Ipswich, is inscribed: "I sound the ravaging of enemy strongholds under Marlborough's leadership". The initial letters providing the date: "*Marlburio Duce Castra Cano Vasta Inimicis*".

On the bells of Stratford St. Mary and Ubbeston are the rare and curious shields of William Culverden of London. His name is made by a rebus of a culver or pigeon with Den above it.

Thomas Gardiner was a Sudbury founder, his earliest bell dating from 1709. At Ickworth his bell states:

> Thos. Gardienr he me did cast,
> I'll sing his praise unto the last.

He worked on until 1759.

Ipswich was the scene of the labours of John Darbie, whose Suffolk bells date from 1648 and end at 1691. His output exceeds that of Miles Graye the elder.

Of these bell castings it suffices to say that our two famous Suffolk ironfounders produced at least one each: Ransomes and Sims the tenor at Tattingstone in 1853; and Garretts' of Leiston for their parish church in 1884.

Munro Cautley points out a very interesting feature of Suffolk bell frames. The wooden pins are driven in from the outside. As the outer members of the frames are usually only a few inches from the walls, it becomes obvious that these frames were erected before the walls were carried up, thus making them of equal date with the towers.

Here follow a few bell inscriptions in alphabetical order.

Cavendish, 1779.

> 1 I mean to make it understood
>   Although I'm little yet I'm good.
> 2 If you have a judicious ear
>   You'l own my voice is sweet and clear
> 3 Music is medicine to the mind
> 4 Peace and good neighbourhood
> 5 Our voices shall in consort ring
>   In honour both to God & King

Dalham, St. Mary, 1627.

> I am the second in degree
> And will in tune and time agree.

> I am the third and you shall hear
> Me beare my part and sound most cleere

Middleton, Holy Trinity, 1779.

> In Wedlock's bands all ye who join
>   With hands your hearts unite
> So shall our tuneful tongues combine
>   To laud the nuptial rite.

Stonham Aspall, St. Lambert.

> At proper times my voice I'll raise
> Unto my benefactor's praise.

Sudbury, All Saints, cast 1576, recast 1875.

> I toll the Funeral knell
> I ring the Festal Day
> I mark the fleeting hours
> And chime the Church to pray.

Sudbury, St. Gregory, 1774.

> Ye Ringers all that prize
> Your health and happiness
> Be sober, merry wise
> And you'll the same possess.

6

Folk-lore

About, about, in reel and rout
The death-fires danced at night;
The water, like a witch's oils,
Burnt green, and blue and white.

Coleridge.

Suffolk is naturally rich in folk-lore, that is customs, beliefs, superstitions, cures and the like. I do not suppose it differs from any other county in these respects, but, as Forby in his *Vocabulary of East Anglia* has pointed out, there is an absence of gloomy legends, because the aspect of the county is milder than many, with an absence of high lands, caves and rocks in which evil spirits delight to dwell. Moreover, the county has been well documented on the subject with a volume all its own, published in 1893 by the Lady Evelina Camilla Gurdon for the Folk-lore Society.

Agricultural myths head the list with weeds, which is only natural in such an intensely farming country. These were considered natural to the ground, in the sense that the ground originated them, because the ground had been cursed as a punishment for man's disobedience. They were natural to the ground in the sense that they spring eternal from the ground itself, not from seeds. Charlock and the corn poppy were the chief, the latter a beautiful sight, though not to the farmer. P. J. O. Trist tells of an old farmer at Waldringfield who remembered the time when it was difficult to find enough wheat to tie up the poppies at harvest.

Stones were an easy second, because the land produced them. All the same women and children were engaged in picking them off the fields year by year.

Toads were generally evil and to be abhorred. They, with

spiders, sucked the poison of the earth. So wrote Shakespeare in *Richard II*.

> Weeping, smiling, greet I thee, my earth:
> Feed not thy Soverign's foes my gentle earth;
> But let thy spiders that suck up thy venom,
> And heavy gaited toads, lie in their way.

Then the small masses of white frothy matter seen on weeds and wild flowers were frog-spit, toad-spit or snake-spit. And the house leeks that grew on old tiled roofs were a splendid defence against lightning.

The raven was an ominous bird, and if it paid one a visit accompanied by a croak, it was a sign of death in the family. Robins were highly protected as they boded ill to any who should deal roughly with them, take their eggs, etc. As for killing one, that boded terrible consequences. "You must not take robin's eggs; if you do you will get your legs broken," was a saying in Suffolk. And accordingly you will never find their eggs on the long strings of which boys are so proud.

"How badly you write," I said one day to a boy in our parish school; "your hand shakes so that you can't hold the pen steady. Have you been running hard, or anything of that sort?" "No," replied the lad, "it always shakes. I once had a robin die in my hand; and they say that if a robin dies in your hand, it will always shake." (This is from "Suffolk", in C. W. J. Chamber's *Book of Days*.)

The belief in ill-luck through bringing small birds' eggs into a house is widespread in East Anglia.

> The robin red-breast and the wren
> Are God Almighty's cock and hen;
> The martin and the swallow
> Are the next two birds that follow.

Bees might have a volume written about them, their pernickety ways and temperamental behaviour. It would appear that all the old women kept bees and humoured them like spoilt children. They had to be told of a death, put into mourning; and above all, when starting a hive, they must not be paid for in money. Bees

The herbal flora found in the Suffolk hedgerows

were said to be so sensitive as to leave houses the inmates of which habitually indulged in swearing.

Ladybirds were called Bishop-Barnabees, and were responsible for that pleasant little rhyme for country girls:

> Gowden-bug, Gowden-bug, fly away home;
> Yar house is bahnt deown an yar children all gone.
> Fly to the East, and fly to the West,
> Fly to the home that you like best.

Rooks building near a house was a sign of prosperity, but if they left a place it was a bad sign. It would appear that they possessed wonderful instinct especially foresight into the future, and trees left bare have been known to be blown down. The counting of magpies must have been universal. Crickets brought good luck into the house, though if they left hurriedly it was a very bad omen. But folks had nothing to say about black beetles.

Horses were credited with being able to see ghosts, while the howling of dogs was a sign of ill-luck. Of the latter I can recall the eeriness of the sound, when nights were so still and sound travelled far. To hear a dog barking or howling in the distance, as one lay in bed, was distinctly ominous.

The feathers in a feather-bed were not without question, possibly that was why a Lincolnshire feather-bed was a positive heirloom. This was because if one contained doves' or pigeons' feathers, it was of no use, and a woman would refuse to be confined on such a one. It meant a hard death. Usually these old feather-beds were the pride of anyone connected with farm life, and were made of goose feathers for preference.

Then, of course, there was that little rhyme much in use in my mother's day:

> If the viper could hear and the slow-worm could see,
> Then England from serpents would never be free.

Customs about the birth of a child, or superstitions about new-born children abounded. The youngest child in the family was known as a 'pin-basket'. Forby says the origin of so odd a name was probably this. When the birth of a first child was expected, and a basket of childbed linen had to be provided, the female friends of the expectant mother made contributions to it, principally of their own needlework, such as laced caps, cambric robes, silk wrappers, etc. Among them a large pincushion was always conspicuous. It was generally made of white satin, trimmed with a silk or silver fringe with tassels at the corners. It was always the work of some unmarried lady, to whom it afforded an exercise of her taste and ingenuity in disposing pins of different lengths, inserted into the cushion only by the points, in various and fanciful forms, so as to produce some resemblance of a light and elegant basket. These pins were never drawn out for use. The most sensible and experienced nurses would think that a thing of ill omen. On the birth of the last child it would seem to fall to him or her as a sort of heirloom.

Babies born in the chime hours—three, six, nine and twelve—had the faculty of seeing spirits and could not be bewitched.

Holy Baptism had its signs and tokens. If the child cried at the pouring on of the water it was a good sign, if it did not it would die, being too good for this world.

Cures for various complaints were numerous, and in many cases efficacious. The more one gathers information of the empirical knowledge of the so-called doctors of the times, the more one realizes the harm they did. Quackery was indeed their chief and ignorant method. In all probability they killed far more than they cured. If one fell into their hands there was no escape. It is small wonder that the 'wise women' proliferated.

There were cures for whooping cough, agues, bleeding at the nose—which they did their utmost to staunch, whereas the doctors bled folks at the earliest and least opportunity. Toothache, warts, wens, burns, typhus fever, rheumatism, cramp, and even nightmare, were all within their power to deal with.

One curious belief was that a lady who by marriage did not change her name was the best of persons to administer medicines, since no remedy given by her would ever fail to cure. It was thought that an infant would cut its teeth more easily if wearing a necklace of ordinary glass beads, or even one of seeds strung together. And a charm against bleeding of the nose was to wear a skein of scarlet thread. A woman in Woodbridge wore a piece of red velvet round her neck for the same purpose. After all, red is, or was, a protective colour.

Bad eyesight must have plagued many, but rainwater collected on Holy Thursday was considered to have healing properties for this purpose. The number of place-names, such as Brightwell, Elmswell, Herringswell, Sizewell, all suggest holy wells with healing properties in the realm of ophthalmia. An old man at Woodbridge, aged 85, used to rise at 5.30 a.m. each morning to bathe his eyes in the 'dag' or dew, to do them good. He suffered from cataract.

Wart-curing and burn-curing were carried on by those gifted with the powers necessary. Moreover they worked according to methods handed down.

It was different at Lowestoft, where one of the 'fishermen's cures' was black beer for backache, called by them 'Norway beer'. Another cure in which fishermen had great faith was a Mrs. Love's ointment. This was made up by an old lady living in Denmark Road, who prepared and boxed it up in her kitchen. It was a most effective cure for poisoned fingers and hands caused by weavers and other poisonous fish. It was also extremely good for sea-hands, hands that had been split by constant hauling of ropes.

They also were great advocates of 'Dutch drops'. Hardly a fishing craft sailed out of the port without this stuff in someone's ditty box. A few drops on sugar was considered a sure cure for colds, bronchial troubles, lumbago and backache. Sometimes it was put in a basin with boiling water and the vapour inhaled to clear the head. It was a thick, black, treacly fluid.

Brandon held a good deal of folk-lore, which was only natural considering its antiquity. As recently as 1892 a Brandon woman was missing, feared drowned, so the Thetford Navigation Superintendent rowed down the Little Ouse with a policeman slowly beating a drum. It was alleged that if they came to any part of the river where there was a dead body a difference in the sound of the drum would be noticeable.

Villagers near the upper part of the Little Ouse believe that if you catch a running toad ('natterjack'), put it in an ants' nest until all the flesh is gone and then put the bones in a running stream, one of them will stand upright. Take this out and with it you can do what you like—make yourself into a witch or wizard.

For curing warts, a piece of bacon was stolen, used to rub on a

The Buttercross, Bungay

wart, and then buried. As the fat wasted away so would the wart. One man sold his warts to a charmer for a farthing, another counted his eighty-four at intervals until they vanished. A cure for hiccoughs was to put a forefinger in each ear and drink from a glass of water; and for chilblains to run barefoot in the snow.

Tench was a fish with a healing property, so it was alleged that a pike, when wounded, would rub up against it as a cure. A snake's avel (skin) worn under the hat was a cure for headache. Pimples could be cured by rubbing them with a gold wedding ring. 'Old sows' (woodlice) swallowed as pills were efficacious in cases of scrofula. A cure for rickets or rupture in very young children was to pass them naked through a cleft sapling ash tree.

Death omens abounded. If a corpse is supple after death it bodes another death in the family before long. If a grave was open on a Sunday, another would be dug before the end of the week. Yew was a fruitful precursor of death if brought into the house at Christmas. The screech of an owl flying past the window of a sick room signified that death was near. Fires produced coffin sparks, and candles winding sheets; while the ebbing tide of the sea prompted the immortal passage voiced by Dickens.

> Tide flowing is feared, for many a thing,
> Great danger to such as be sick, it doth bring;
> Sea ebb, by long ebbing, some respite doth give,
> And sendeth good comfort to such as shall live.

And so we might go on, until it appears quite remarkable that any of our ancestors escaped to leave any record of themselves.

If a swarm of bees alight either on a dead tree or dead bough of a living tree near the house, or if a bird flies indoors or even taps at the window with its beak, or if the clock loses a stroke or refuses to go properly, or if the cuckoo's first note be heard in bed, or if a light be shut up in a room or closet at the time unoccupied, then there will be a death in the family in a short time. The picking of green bloom or May blossom means death to the head of the family into which it is brought; or if an apple or pear tree blooms twice in the year, the same catastrophe is brought about. If you see four crows in your path, or a snake enters your room, or if the cuckoo gives his note from a dead tree, it means coming death to a relative.

Fairies were known as 'frairies' or 'Pharisees' in old Suffolk, and they are certainly a relief from morbid tokens, ghosts and headless horses. Their presence is not surprising when you realize that villages such as Woolpit, literally 'wolves' pit', from which came the Green Children of old romance, or Elveden, otherwise the 'elves' or fairies' den', are to be found in the county. Someone writing in 1903 had conversed with a very old woman who, as a child, had heard the elfin music issuing from that fairies' dell. She firmly believed the horses of anyone who passed the dell could have been bewitched by them, as it was near the roadside.

Fairy loaves were quite common in cottage fireplaces. They were fossilized sea urchins. It was alleged that any house possessing them would never lack bread. They were usually black-leaded with the hearth. With these, of course, went fairy butter, a substance to be found on furze and broom.

It was customary to place a plate of salt on the breast of a corpse and for villagers and children to be called in to view the body. This custom was continued well within living memory.

Headless spectres were quite common. In the village of Acton a legend, current not many years ago, was that on certain unspecified occasions, the park gates flew open at midnight "withouten hands" and a carriage drawn by four spectral horses and accompanied by headless grooms and outriders proceeded rapidly from the park to a spot called 'the nursery corner', where they inconsequentially disappeared. I suppose every village possessed Old Shuck the Black Dog, and some had actually seen him. Usually he had eyes that burned like a flame and lacked nothing in the telling.

Then they would butter a cat's paws to keep it at home if moving to a new house. But the sneezing of a cat was a sign that the family of the owner would soon have colds.

A bride on her wedding day should wear:

> Something old
> Something new,
> Something borrowed,
> Something blue.

Of the weather:

Evening red, and morning grey
Sends the traveller on his way;
But evening grey and morning red,
Sends the traveller wet to bed.

Hopkins the witch-finder went on his circuit and was responsible for the death of many a poor old Suffolk woman—and man, for that matter. For example John Lowes or Lewis, vicar of Brandeston, instituted 6th May 1596, was "after he had been here about 50 years, and 80 years of age, accused of Witchcraft and swam in the Castle ditch at Framlingham". It sounds more like Nazi Germany or what we hear of Russia. Hopkins kept the poor old man awake several days and nights until he was delirious and confessed. He was hanged, but, to make sure of some sort of Christian burial, he read the service over himself as he approached the scene of execution. It was thought he might have been rather cantankerous, and so unscrupulous neighbours swore him away. A more degraded spectacle of malice and hatred never shadowed the annals of religious fanaticism. What is more, belief in witch-craft was held by persons such as Wesley.

"Everything has an end and a pudding has two." In explanation of this Forby observes that our Suffolk puddings are not round, but long; they are sometimes called leg-puddings, from their resemblance to the human leg. Major Moore in his *Vocabulary* lamented the demise of the long pudding, which he considered was vastly superior to the round one. However, in High Suffolk in those days the poke pudding was still held in high esteem. A poke was a bag, and a poke-cart was the miller's cart laden with pokes of flour belonging to his customers. The oven bird was the long-tailed titmouse that built a nest like a poke. It was also known as a pudding-poke's nest.

Blaxhall is noted for fine farming and also for one of those boulder stones around which all kinds of legends have been woven. Such as the one at Lowestoft, known as the Witch's Stone, that goes down to the sea beach to bathe when it hears midnight strike. There was also the Devil's Stone at St. Mary's, Bungay, around which the children danced seven times on a certain day in the year and then looked for the devil to appear.

7

Some Early Visitors
and their Impressions

The Poetry of Earth is never dead:
When all the birds are faint with the hot sun,
And hide in cooling trees, a voice will run
From Hedge to hedge about the new-mown mead.

                                        Keats

Suffolk in the early days must have been somewhat of an enigma
to the outside world. Its very insular position would suggest this,
with roads, Roman roads at that, leading nowhere. Besides,
visitors were looked upon with suspicion, an attitude which has
persisted until only yesterday★. However, some did venture into
this wonderful enclosure, particularly so as many Suffolk fortunes
were made in London itself, and names such as Seckford Street,
Berners Street and Drury Lane, even Hyde Park are all from
Suffolk families. Moreover, the first Royal Exchange was built
of Battisford oaks.

The visitors of note to be quoted saw things from their own
point of view.

The first was Miss Celia Fiennes, grand-daughter of the first
Viscount Saye and Sele, who kept a diary of her travels and called
it *Through England on a Side Saddle in the time of William and Mary*.
She was a Nonconformist and rejoiced in noting the number of
'Dissenters' meetings she met, but was also out to notice the
curious. In outlook she was very much akin to Defoe, and visited
Suffolk on a tour from London through East Anglia to Ely.

Celia starts off with noticing that the distance between Colchester and Ipswich is 18 miles, but she obviously came into

★ Yesterday: writing in 1970, Allan Jobson meant the 1950s rather than the
1930s or earlier.

Suffolk from Dedham, passing over a wooden bridge "pretty large with timber rails of which they build their bridges in these parts". When she gets into the county, probably the way the Romans came, she notes the land is not so rich as in Essex, where the "meadows and groundes" had "great burden of grass and corn".

She notes that Ipswich is a very clean town and much bigger than Colchester. It "has 12 churches, their streets of a good size well pitch'd with small stones, a good Market Cross railed in. I was there on Saturday which is their market day and saw they sold their butter by the pint, 20 ounces for 6 pence, and often 5d or 4d they make it up in a mold just in the shape of a pint pot and so sell it." (I have one of these moulds. In Cambridge they sold butter by the yard.)

She informs us the market cross had some good carvings, with the figure of Justice on top. What a pity that was destroyed. But as far as she was concerned there were only three or four good houses in the town. Of these the chief to note was Christchurch Mansion, occupied by the Earl of Hereford "that married one of Mr. Norborns Daughters that was killed by Sir Thomas Montgomery". Naturally she goes into a detailed description of the house, noting it has a "Billyard Room above with as many rooms of State all furnish'd with good things". She ends: "this Town has many Dessenters in it", notably Quakers.

The town gave her the impression that it was a little disregarded, and by inquiry she found it to be

thro' pride and sloth, for tho' the sea would bear a ship of 300 tons up quite to the key and the ships of the first rate can ride within two miles of the town, yet they make no advantage thereof by any sort of manufacture, which they might do as well as Colchester and Norwich, so that the ships that bring coals goes light away; neither do they address themselves to victuals or provide ships, they have a little dock where formerly they built ships of 2 or 300 ton, but now little or nothing is minded save a little fishing for the supply of the town.

Then I went to Woodbridge 7 miles, mostly lanes enclosed country; this is a little Market town but has a great meeting for the Dissenters [Quakers, to wit the bankers Alexander and Co.] thence to Wickham 5 miles more, but these are all long miles.

The Cupola House, Bury St. Edmunds

Thence to Saxmundham . . . this is a pretty bigg market town, the wayes are pretty deep, mostly lanes very little common; I passed by severall Gentlemens seates.

The next place of note was evidently Blythburgh:

where is the remains of the walls of an Abbey and there is still a fine church, all carved in stone hollow work one tier above another to the tower that ascends not very high but very finely carv'd also . . . thence I passed some woods and little villages of a few scattered houses, and generally the people here are able to give so bad directions that passengers are at a loss what aime to take, they know scarce 3 miles from their home, and mete them where you will, enquire how farre which is the distance from their own houses to that place; I saw at a distance as I descended some of the hills a large place that look'd nobly and stood very high like a large town; they told me it was called either Stowle [Southwold] or Nole I cannot tell which.

. . . to Beckle [Beccles] . . . this is a little market town but its the third biggest town in the County of Suffolk, Ipswich, Berry and this; here was a good big Meeting place at least 400 hearers and they have a good minister one Mr. Killinghall, he is a young man but seemed very serious, I was there on the Lords day; Sir Robert Rich is a great supporter of them and contributed to the building the Meeting place, which is very neate, he has a good house (Roos Hall) at the end of the towne being old timber and plaster work . . . there is a pretty bigg Market Cross and a great big market kept, there is a handsome stone built church and a very good publick Minister whose name is Armstrong he preaches very well; they say notwithstanding the town is a sad Jacobite town; this chooses no parliament men [not a parliamentary borough].

At the Towns end one passes over the river Waveney on a wooden bridge railed with timber and so you enter Norfolk . . . the ordinary people both in Suffolk and Norfolk knitt much and spin, some with rock and fusoe as the French does, others at their wheels out in the streets and lanes one passes.

After a short time she returns to Suffolk: "Next day I went to Euston Hall which was the Lord Arlingtons and by his only daughters marriage with the Duke of Grafton is his sons by her, its two miles from Thetford; it stands in a large park 6 miles about, the house is a Roman H of brick."

Her description of Breckland is interesting: ". . . and passed over perfect down champion country just like Salisbury Plaine, and the winds have a pretty power here and blows strongly in the winter not well to be endured".

So to St. Edmundsbury: "... the Market Cross has a dyal and a lanthorn on the top, and there being another pretty house close to it [Cupola House] high built with such a tower and lanthorn also ... this high house is an apothecarys ... he showed me a curiousity of an Herball all written out with every sort of tree and herb dyed and cut out and pasted on the leaves—it was a Doctor of Physicks work that left him as a Legacy at his death; it was a fine thing and would have delighted me severall dayes but I was passant ... there are many Descenters in the town 4 Meeting places with the Quakers and Anabaptists."

Defoe comes next. He set out on 3rd April 1722 going eastward, and arrived at Harwich harbour. His first note is about Landguard Fort, which "stands out so far into the sea upon a point of a sand or shoal, which runs out towards the Essex side, as it were layes over the mouth of the haven like a blind to it, and our surveyors of the county affirm it to be in the county of Essex".

He states that the country round Ipswich is applied chiefly to corn, of which a great quantity is shipped off to London, also to Holland when the market is favourable. His comment on Ipswich is much more favourable than Celia Fiennes', because he finds a great deal of good company here although there are not so many gentry as at Bury. He considers the cause is the frequent conversation with those that have been abroad. He goes on: "I take this town to be one of the most agreeable places in England," and gives six reasons:

1. Good houses at very easy rents.
2. An airy, clean and well governed town.
3. Very agreeable and improving company almost of every kind.
4. A wonderful plenty of all manner of provisions, whether flesh or fish, and very good of the kind.
5. Those provisions very cheap, so that a family may live cheaper here than in any town in England of its bigness, within such a small distance of London.
6. Easy passage to London, either by land or water, the coach going through to London in a day.

Naturally he calls attention to the fine seat and park called Christchurch. Also that the steeple of the town church had been blown down causing much damage. "They send two members to Parliament—Sir William Thompson, Recorder of London, and Colonel Negus, Deputy-master of the horse to the King."

Defoe notes there were some very curious things to see in Ipswich, although some superficial writers had missed them. "Dr. Beeston, an eminent physician, began a few years ago, a physick garden adjoining his house . . . and as he is particularly curious and . . . exquisitely skilled in botanic knowledge, so he has not only diligent, but successful too, in making a collection of rare and exotic plants such as are scarce to be equalled in England."

From Ipswich he went to Hadleigh to "see the place where that famous martyr and pattern of charity and religious zeal in Queen Mary's time, Dr. Rowland Taylor, was put to death".

Thence to Sudbury: "I know nothing for what this town is remarkable except for being very populous and very poor." And so to Long Melford: ". . . and a very long one it is". Which naturally leads to Bury St. Edmunds, ". . . a town of which other writers have talked very largely, and perhaps a little too much". However, ". . . the beauty of the town consists in the number of gentry who dwell in or near it, the sweet air they breathe in and the pleasant country they have to go about in".

Woodbridge comes next, remarkable for it being an outlet for the produce of High Suffolk in butter and corn exported to London. "The butter is barralled or often pickled up in small casks and sold, not in London only, but I have known a firkin of Suffolk butter sent to the West Indies and brought back to England again, and has been perfectly good and sweet as at first."

His description of Orford is quaint: "Orford was once a good town, but is decayed, and as it stands on the land side of the river, the sea daily throws up more land to it and falls off itself from it, as if it was resolved to disown the place and that it should be a sea port no longer." "From Albro' to Dunwich there are no towns of note. . . . This town is a testimony to the decay of public things:

By numerous examples we may see
That towns and cities die, as well as we."

However, Dunwich still retained "some share of trade as particularly the shipping of butter, cheese and corn".

He found no business at Southwold save the fishing for herrings and sprats "which they cure by the help of smoke as they do at Yarmouth". However, it was here that he observed the swallows "first land when they come to visit us, and here they may be said to embark for their return when they go back into warmer climates". It was here he noticed swarms of them sitting on the church and the houses, and asked why they waited. "I enquired of a grave gentleman: 'O Sir' says he 'you may see the reason, the wind is off the sea . . . the weather being too calm, or the wind contrary, they are waiting for a gale, for they are all wind-bound'."

High Suffolk, he notes, is full of rich feeding grounds, and remarkable as being the first where the feeding and fattening of cattle and sheep with turnips was practised in England. He then goes on into great detail about the traffic of turkeys to London, since these were more bred in Suffolk and Norfolk than all the rest of England.

He was informed that 300 droves of turkeys were driven on foot, over Stratford Bridge that crossed the Stour, each drove containing 500 birds. Geese also were made to travel on foot, feeding *en route* on the stubble after harvest. Later a carriage was invented of four storeys high into which the birds were packed. "The horses in this new fashioned voiture go two abreast . . . but no perch below as a coach, but they are fastened together by a piece of wood lying cross-wise upon their necks by which they are kept even and together, and the driver sits on the top of the cart, like as in the public carriage for the army etc."

We now come to William Cobbett and his *Rural Rides*, made at the end of 1821, and his *Eastern Tour* of 1830. "The land all along to Bury St. Edmunds is very fine; but no trees worth looking at. . . . The farming all along to Norwich is very good. The land clean, and everything done in a masterly manner."

Beccles, he thought, was a very pretty place, "has water

meadows near it, and is situated amidst fine lands. . . . The churches prove that the people of Norfolk and Suffolk were always a superior people in point of wealth. . . . The great drawbacks on the beauties of these counties are, their flatness and their want of woods."

His description of Ipswich almost amounts to a panegyric:

On the 19th. I proceeded to Ipswich, not imagining it to be the fine populous and beautiful place that I found it to be. . . . It is the great outlet for the immense quantities of corn grown in this most productive county, and by farmers the most clever that ever lived. . . . Immense quantities of flour are sent from the town. The windmills on the hills of the vicinage are so numerous that I counted whilst standing in one place, no less than seventeen. They are all painted or washed white; the sails are black; it was a fine morning, the wind was brisk, and the twirling together added greatly to the beauty of the scene, which, having the broad and beautiful arm of the sea on the one hand, and the fields and meadows, studded with farm-houses, on the other, appeared to me the most beautiful sight of the kind that I had ever beheld. The town and its churches were down in the dell before me.

He continues in the same strain, finding views that a painter might crave, farmhouses all white, barns and everything so snug, stocks of turnips abundant everywhere; sheep and cattle in fine order; wheat all drilled; ploughmen so expert with furrows of a quarter of a mile long, as straight as a line. In short, here was everything to delight the eye and to make people proud of their country. "I have always found Suffolk farmers great boasters of their superiority over others; and I must say that it is not without reason."

Travelling from Ipswich through Needham Market and Stowmarket to Bury St. Edmunds, he remarked that he did not see one single instance of paper or rags supplying the place of glass in any windows.

To conclude an account of Suffolk and not sing the praise of Bury St. Edmunds, would offend every creature of Suffolk birth: even at Ipswich, when I was praising that place, the very people of that town asked me if I did not think Bury St. Edmunds the nicest town in the world. Meet them wherever you will, they have all the same

Weavers' cottages, Lavenham

boast; and indeed, as a town in itself, it is the neatest place that ever was seen. It is airy, it has several fine open places in it . . . and it is so clean and so neat that nothing can equal it in that respect.

After all, what is the reflection now called for? It is that this fine county, for which nature has done all that she can do, soil, climate, sea-ports, people; everything that can be done, and an internal government, civil and ecclesiastical, the most complete in the world, wanting nothing but to be left alone, to make every soul in it as happy as people can be upon earth.

However, with the poor, there was a contentment as envisaged in the poetry of Bloomfield, and there was a squalor and a fatalism as portrayed by Crabbe. The former could write:

> On thy calm joys with what delight I dream
> Thou dear green valley of my native stream!

While Crabbe wrote of his compatriots:

> a wild, amphibious race,
> With sullen woe display'd in every face:
> Who far from civil arts and social fly,
> And scowl at strangers with suspicious eye.

No portrait of Suffolk would be complete without reference to that wonderful man and ardent traveller, who was such a shrewd as well as a truthful observer of the many men he came in contact with and the places he visited. But he was a very different person to those we have just been considering. John Wesley did not come into Suffolk for the purpose of observation but to preach. The churches closed their doors to him but he was not discouraged and, in that famous phrase, looked upon all the world as his parish as he went on his way. Only once does he appear to have visited Ipswich, when he was *en route* from Colchester to Norwich, and this is what he wrote in his journal under the date 13th October 1790: "We set out early, but found no horses at Cobbock [Copdock]; so that we were obliged to go round by Ipswich, and wait there half an hour."

Samuel Tymms, in his handbook of Bury St. Edmunds, states that the first Methodist chapel was built in St. Mary's Square in 1811, upon the site of a smaller one, in which John Wesley had repeatedly preached.

One thinks of him as jogging along on his ambling horse, his little library safely in his saddle bags; possibly reading as he went, and finding a meal in the hedgerows. He was a romantic figure, and one wonders how he liked the Suffolk roads and the Suffolk scene. Crabbe, who detested new light and sudden conversions, was a great admirer of the itinerant preacher.

Wesley was at Yarmouth on 10th October 1764, when he was desired to go to Lowestoft. The use of a large place had been offered, which would contain an abundance of people. But when he arrived the host had changed his mind, so he preached in the open air. Here he found ". . . a wilder congregation I have not seen; but the Bridle was in their teeth. All attended: and a considerable part seemed to understand something of what was spoken; nor did any behave uncivily when I had done: and I believe a few did not lose their labour."

Lowestoft figures several times in his journal.

1776, Tuesday, Nov. 19th. I opened the new preaching-house at Lowestofft; a new and lightsome building. It was thoroughly filled with deeply attentive hearers.

Wednesday 20th. Mr. Fletcher preached in the morning, and I at two in the afternoon. It then blew a thorough storm, so that it was hard to walk or stand, the wind being ready to take us off our feet. It drove one of the boats which were on the strand from its moorings out to sea. Three men were in it, who looked for nothing every moment but to be swallowed up. But presently five stout men put off in another open boat, and, rowing for life, overtook them, and brought them safe to land.

Thursday 21st. I preached at Beccles. A duller place I have seldom seen.

1779, Monday, January 15th. I went to Norwich in the stage-coach with two very disagreeable companions, called a gentleman and gentlewoman, but equally ignorant, insolent, lewd and profane.

Thursday 18th. I preached at Lowestofft, where is a great awakening, especially among youth and children; several of whom, between twelve and sixteen years of age, were a pattern to all about them.

1782, Thursday, October 23rd. I went on to Lowestofft, which is at present far the most comfortable place in the Circuit.

1788, Thursday, October 23rd. We went to Lowestofft where the people have stood firm from the beginning.

1789, Monday, October 6th., I preached at Loddon, North Cove, and Lowestofft. When I came into the town it blew a storm; and many cried out "So it always does when he comes." But it fell as suddenly as it rose; for God heard the prayer.

1790, Friday, October 15th. I went to Lowestofft to a steady, loving, united society. The more strange it is that they neither increase nor decrease in number.

Wesley was then 88 years old, and, with none of the pains, conscious of the infirmity of age, of which he says he had not felt a symptom for 86 years. This was probably his last visit to Lowestoft, and it was on this occasion that Crabbe, the poet, heard and saw him with his long white locks, supported in the pulpit by two young ministers. It was then he applied to himself the lines of Cowley's *Anacreon*:

> Oft am I by women told
> Poor Anacreon! thou grow'st old;
> See, thine hairs are falling all,
> Poor Anacreon! how they fall!
> Whether I grow old or no,
> By these signs I do not know;
> But this I need not to be told,
> 'Tis time to live if I grow old.

Crabbe was much struck by the beautiful cadence he gave to these lines.

To end the visitors' list we might include this extract from the *Suffolk Garland*. It throws a good deal of light on the times and conditions of life in those days. Suffolk fare was obviously not to be despised by those who lived above stairs in a Georgian England. It has an authentic atmosphere of a vanished world of leisure and privilege. You will notice there is little or no reference to the countryside, which is taken for granted; it is merely a tale of good living and frivolity.

Journal Of a very young Lady's Tour from Canonbury to Aldeburgh, &c. written hastily on the road, as occurrences arose.

LETTER I.   *Sudbury*, Sep. 13th., 1804.

My dear sister P. let me hope that your suavity
Will not take offence at my sport, or my gravity;

In describing my Travels I've much to relate,
And I'm sure you will kindly allow me to prate.
　At length in good time we're to Sudbury come,
And (thanks to friend M—) have got a good room;
Good lamb, and good ducks, good pye, and good wine;
On which it is soon our intention to dine.
　We've been strolling an hour, to survey this old town;
One street we walk'd up, another walk'd down;
The barges examin'd, and new navigation,
Not the first in the world, nor the first in the nation;
And are safely return'd, without any affright,
To our snug little inn; and shall stay here all night.
And now we are thinking of supper d'ye see,
So no more at present, my dear sister P.

LETTER II.   *Ipswich*, Sep. 14th.
　At the mansion arrived, how delighted was I
Such beautiful gardens and grounds to espy!
We examin'd the dairy, the orchard, the grapery.
And escap'd without injuring at all my fine drapery;
Rich cakes and ripe fruits form'd our morning regale;
Whilst new milk was thought pleasanter far than old ale;
And, when with reluctance we mounted the chaise,
I could not help singing out loud in its praise.
We brought away stores of provision and fruit,
And such as an epicure's palate might suit:
Two brace of young birds, and a fine sort of plum;
A sack-full of pears all as sound as a drum;
Cob-nuts, golden pippins, grapes, and mulberries galore,
Pearmains, red streaks, with nonp'reils, and many sorts more.
　Just before we pass'd over the Brett's purling rill,
We saw Kersey church on the slope of a hill;
Then to Hadleigh proceeded, which much we approv'd,
Secur'd some refreshment, and then onward mov'd.
　At Hintlesham nothing appear'd that was frightful,
The country's delicious, the roads are delightful;
Such beautiful turnips sure never were seen,
(The roots are cream white, and the tops are dark green);
And I fear you will think me a mere London bumkin,
When I tell you how much I was pleas'd with a pumkin.
At Sproughton (you'll scarce think it worth the remarking)
The pigs were all grunting, the dogs were all barking;

Mr Collinson's grounds called the Chantry are pleasant,
An excellent haunt for hares, partridge, and pheasant.
And now, to make short of this travelling story,
At Ipswich we're landed and I'm in my glory;
At a table well stor'd with ham, chicken, and pudding,
And a house that one scarcely can fail to be good in!

LETTER III. *Ipswich*, Sep. 15th.

Whilst at Ipswich abiding, you'll expect not much news;
I shall not talk of rubbers, of snugs, or fine views.
The churches are numerous, the market place spacious;
The streets are well pav'd, and the shops are capacious.
This morning to Woodbridge I went with a beau,
To smell at the mud whilst the water was low:
Yet the ride was quite cheerful, the country quite charming,
And the red coats, tho' numerous are not much alarming.

LETTER IV. *Ipswich*, Sept. 16th.

Being Sunday, we've all been to church, you'll be sure,
Where the prayers were well read, and the doctrine was pure.

LETTER V. *Aldeburgh*, Sep. 17th.

Permit me, dear sister, to greet you once more,
Not from shady retreats, but from Aldeburgh's rough shore.
Thro' Woodbridge and Wickham our post horses rattled,
Whilst the ride we enjoy'd, and incessantly prattled.
'Twas a custom in Suffolk, I've heard trav'llers tell,
To drink health to all friends who live round Wickham well;
But I'm sure sister Sarah was ready to jump,
When she found the old well was transform'd to a pump.
At last passing Snape church, on Snape common, believe me,
To a number of sticks my attention directed.
Which for May-poles, she said, had been lately erected.
But this was mere joking, I very well knew,
For presently many tall ships pass'd in view;
And you cannot but guess how my heart was in motion,
When at length we obtain'd a full view of the ocean.
And now at the Lion behold us again,
Where for two nights at least we've agreed to remain;
And shall great havock make with the Aldeburgh soals,
Which here in fine seasons they catch in large shoals;

And for lobsters, so plentiful here do they buy them,
I believe in my heart I shall venture to try them.

LETTER VI. *Aldeburgh*, Sep. 18th.
    This morning to rambling was wholly applied;
On the beach we first walk'd till disturb'd by the tide;
Then we mounted the terrace, a beautiful place,
Whence the views are immense o'er the Ocean's wide space:

LETTER VII. *Aldeburgh*, Sep. 19th.
    At length, my dear sister, your father's young daughter
Has fairly been plung'd head and heels in the water.
Having made up my mind that I'd have a good dip,
I went into a waggon that swims like a ship;
But of one point 'tis needless to have the least doubt,
As fast as I possibly could I crept out;
And, shaking my ears like a tragedy queen,
I could hardly imagine I'd really been in.
    But now the scene changes, and homeward we pace,
Recollecting the vestige of each charming place;
Till at Ipswich once more we're arriv'd full of glee,
And now for the present farewell to the sea!

LETTER VIII. *Ipswich*, Sep. 20th.
Our next route, my dear sister, 's intended for Harwich,
So behold us at Ipswich remounting our carriage;
But, as travellers must frequently find to their cost,
There's a proverb call'd Reckoning more fast than your host.
    As Stoke Bridge is repairing, the road lies thro' the river,
Where, when the tide rises, the ford's not very clever;
And by prudent observers 'tis well understood,
That 'tis not very pleasant to *stick in the mud*;
So we tried the old bridge, and, as sure as a fiddle,
We flounder'd before we got half to the middle;
Yet, as money does all things, the workmen were willing
To prepare us a road, if we gave them a shilling.
This obstacle conquer'd, we drove on like Jehu,
Till Freston's old tower appear'd full in our view;
The Orwell's fring'd banks like enchantment look'd gay,
And gave a new zest to the charms of the day.
    Next to Shotley proceeding, we reach'd Shotley Ferry,
Where we find some good brandy to make our hearts merry;

But the worst of it is (tho' we laugh and are glad,)
Not a passage-boat here is, alas! to be had;
But we shall not be kept very long in suspence,
For a small two-oared wherry is soon going hence.
   But now we're at Harwich, and thankful am I,
Our inn's the Three Cups, and our dinner draws nigh.
But first for a walk to survey this old borough,
To peep at the church, and the church-yard go thorough.
On the opposite shore Landguard Fort boldly stands,
Well secur'd by Britannia's invincible bands.
Long, long may our Monarch the honour retain
Of being king of the Islands that govern the Main.

8

Agriculture

Ah, blest beyond all bliss the husbandmen, did they but know their happiness! On whom, far from the clash of arms, the most just Earth showers from her bosom a toilless sustenance.

Georgics

Plough, or plough not, you must pay your rent.

Suffolk through all the centuries has had a great reputation as an agricultural county. It was noted for its enterprise and was described as a land of plenty. It has even been suggested that it began in the years of the Roman occupation. Camden's *Britannia* states it was "full of havens of a fat and fertile soil", and "had most rich and goodly cornfields". This is confirmed by the observations made by the three visitors we have already quoted. Take as an example the village of Mickfield, near Stowmarket, where in the 1879 *Directory* all the inhabitants were farmers.

Arthur Young was the great authority, with his *General View of the Agriculture of the County of Suffolk*, published in 1813. Although born at Westminster he was the son of the rector of Bradfield. He begins with the climate, one of the driest in the kingdom and continues with the soil. "There is not, perhaps a county in the kingdom which contains a greater diversity of soil, or more clearly discriminated. A strong loam, on a clay-marl bottom."

As to the size of farms, those in Suffolk he reckoned large: "and to that circumstance, more perhaps than any other, is to be attributed the good husbandry so commonly found in the county". He accounted Westwood Lodge, Blythburgh, 3,000 acres, as the finest farm in the county.

Turning to implements he instances the Norfolk wheel plough, and the little light swing plough of Suffolk, as the common implements. The latter was good for a depth not exceeding 4 inches.

He notes that Brand, an Essex man, had improved the Suffolk plough and made it of iron. He then goes on to the horse rake drawn by one horse for cleaning spring corn stubbles, instead of the corn dew rake drawn by a man. Then comes the drill roller, which made "little channels four-and-a-half inches asunder, across a clover lay after ploughing; the wheat seed is then sown broadcast and is covered in with a bush harrow".

But the prize bit of mechanism, illustrated, was the extirpator, invented by a Mr. Haywood of Stoke Ash: "The extirpator or scalp plough is drawn by two or three horses. . . . It will work in all lands, and may be handled by any person that knows how to manage a plough." This was to clear the ground of weeds.

"Though the dairy district of Suffolk is extensive, and the number of sheep kept great, yet the arable part of the county is much the most considerable." This leads on to tillage.

Ploughing:

In every part of the county this is done with a pair of horses, conducted with reins by the ploughman; and the quantity of land turned in a day, is an acre upon stiff soils, and from one and a quarter to one and a half on sands.

The ploughmen are remarkable for straight furrows; and also for drawing them by the eye to any object, usually a stick whitened by peeling, either for water cuts, or for new laying out broad ridges, called here stetches; and a favourite amusement is ploughing such furrows, as candidates for a hat, or a pair of briches, given by ale-house keepers, or subscribed among themselves, as a prize for the straightest furrows. The skill of many of them in this work is remarkable.

Since ploughing was the most skilled occupation on the farm, and if the old saying be true that "A man must plough with such oxen as he hath," then Suffolk was fortunate. It possessed not only the oxen but the ploughs also; those vital implements for the production of a good harvest, ploughs invented and brought to perfection by the ingenuity of skilled and enterprising black-smiths and engineers.

The swing plough was invented by John Brand, a blacksmith of Lawford, Essex, who was by all accounts a Suffolk man. He also fitted the plough with a cathead, or copse, and Young went so far as to say it was an improvement and there was no other in

Saxtead Mill, monument to a bygone agricultural age

the kingdom equal to it. Among other things, announced by Young, "he makes an iron swing plough to be drawn by a pair of horses, which much excels any plough I have yet seen, in cutting a regular true furrow, well cleared of the loose moulds, or in turning over grass lands, at the same time that in strength and duration it is far preferable to all".

Another machine was a horse-rake on wheels for raking spring corn stubbles, that would also rake hay. Also a hand-mill for grinding wheat.

William and Hugh Raynbird of Hengrave give a full description of the Norfolk plough. The beam was elevated and made to rest on a bar of wood called the bolster, which crossed the upright standards that formed part of the carriage framing supported by the wheels. The draught chain collared the beam and could be removed easily from the notches, while the small chain served to keep the standards in the upright position. The bolster was made to rise and fall as the plough was required to cut shallower or deeper.

All these wheel ploughs required frequent adjustment as to their wheels, which occasioned loss of time; and, unless the furrows were ploughed beyond the length required, the larger wheel had to be raised at each end of the field just before the plough came out of the furrow. However, the loss of time (a curious expression in those days of long unhurried hours) was overcome by a simple mechanical contrivance invented by yet another Suffolk man, Henry Osborne. It consisted of a lever, the longer end of which reached the handle of the plough, and by this the wheel could be adjusted to any depth. It is to be noted that these ploughs were of the one-handled variety; and this type was peculiar to Norfolk and Suffolk.

Burwell wheat seed was greatly used and dibbling was then in practice: "The ground being rolled with a light barley roller, a man walking backwards on the *flag*, as the furrow slice is called, with a dibber of iron, the handle about three feet long, in each hand, strikes two rows of holes, about four inches from one row to the other, on each flag; and he is followed by three or four children to drop the grains, three, four or five in a hole. . . . A bush-harrow follows to cover it." This led to a little verse sung by the youthful droppers:

> Four seeds in a hole;
> One for the rook, one for the crow,
> One to rot and one to grow.

These irons were designed for corn or beans, the latter having a larger knob at the end. Dibbled wheat was said to grow finer than any other. Cutting out thistles with weeding hooks, is universal, adds Young.

Next comes barley. "The common barley is the only sort I have known cultivated in Suffolk. Barley is everywhere in Suffolk mown, and left loose: the neater method of binding in sheaves, is not practised. The stubbles are dew raked, by men drawing a long iron-toothed rake; but this is better, and much quicker performed by a horse-rake a very effective tool."

Later in date came the Chevallier Barley, which became one of the most popular varieties in England. Its origin was described by a Mr. Sam Dove of Debenham, 1835:

About 10 to 15 years since John Andrews, a labourer had been threshing barley and on his return home at night he complained of his feet being very uneasy. On taking off his shoes he discovered in one of them part of a very fine ear of barley. It struck him as being particularly so, and was careful to have it preserved. He afterwards planted it in his garden and on the following year Dr. and Mrs. Charles Chevallier coming to Andrews' cottage to inspect some repairs going on (the cottage belonged to the Doctor), saw three or four ears of the barley growing, he requested it might be kept for him when ripe. The Doctor sowed a small ridge with the produce thus obtained and kept it by itself until he was able to plant an acre and from this acre the produce was 11½ coombs, now about 9 years since. This was again planted and from the increase thence arising he began to dispose of it and from that time it has been gradually getting into repute. It is now well known in most of the corn markets of the kingdom and also in many parts of the Continent and called after the Doctor's name, the Chevallier Barley.

The discovery of kersey white clover was also a rather romantic find. It has been developed from a small plant found in 1924 growing among a crop of lucerne by Everett Partridge of Witnesham.

Of Oats, "the black, the white, the Tartarian, and the light oat, are the sorts cultivated in Suffolk". Rye: "This grain has gradually given way to the cultivation of wheat, by means of those improvements which in the last fifty years have taken place in so many parts of the kingdom. It is now found only on poor sands."

Beans: "It is difficult to cultivate rich moist soils to full advantage, without the assistance of this plant, which has two qualities of singular importance; first, that of extracting very little from the fertility of the land; and second, preparing better, perhaps, for wheat, than any other crop." Pease: "We have white, blue, grey, and dun, with names of their respective colours. They are generally cut with what is called a pease make, which is half an old scythe fixed in a handle, with which they were rolled into small bundles, called *wads*, as they are cut."

Buck Wheat: "Is, in this county, on the very poorest sands, more common than in many other parts of England; and is, for such soils, a very valuable crop. Harvest, Mown, and gathered loose." Tares: "This plant is generally cultivated to the extent of a few acres; the scale applicable to soiling the horses of the farm; it is not, however, as it ought to be a universal practice." Cole Seed: "There is a considerable quantity of cole-seed sown in all parts of the county; but in the fen district, it is one of the principle crops."

Turnips: "The culture of this plant may justly be estimated the greatest improvement in English husbandry that has been established in the present century. In Suffolk, it has changed the face of the poorer soils, and rendered them more productive to the landlord, the tenant, and the public, than any other system of management, perhaps, that could be devised. . . . The white round Norfolk is preferred; the red round, and the small green round, are known, but the tankard sorts are uncommon." In the cultivation of turnips he refers to Old Midsummer, a sign that the revision of the calendar was not observed in agriculture.

Clover: "After the culture of turnips, the introduction of this plant, as a preparation for wheat, must be esteemed the greatest of modern improvements upon arable lands. It has been cultivated in Suffolk largely beyond the memory of the oldest man; and is, in every branch of its management, perfectly well understood by good farmers." Sanfoin: "This noble plant, the most profitable of all others on the soil it affects, is much cultivated in Suffolk. In the sandy districts, especially the western, it is every where found, though not in the quantity that ought to be sown of it. . . . It requires no other making than once turning the swaths."

Hops: "At Stowmarket and its vicinity, there are about 200 acres of hops, which deserve mention, as an article which is not generally spread through the kingdom. A hop garden will last almost for ever, by renewing the hills that fail, to the amount of about a score annually; but it is reckoned better to grub up and new plant it every twenty or twenty-five years." In fact Suffolk can claim to have been one of the first counties in England to grow hops, which were introduced from the Artois in 1524. Tusser has a rhyme for it:

> The hop for his profit I thus do exalt,
> It strengtheneth drink, and it flavoureth malt,
> And being well brewed, long kept it will last:
> And drawing abide—if ye draw not too fast.

Cabbages: "The cultivation of cabbages is another article which aids not inconsiderably to the agricultural merit of Suffolk. . . . The Rev. Mr. Chevallier had cultivated them with attention for several years; and has found them so very convenient in frost and snow, that he would never be without some, were there no other reason for it." Carrots: "The culture of carrots in the Sandlings, or district within the line formed by Woodbridge, Saxmundham and Orford, but extending to Leiston, is one of the most interesting objects to be met with in the agriculture of Britain . . . they have of late years been cultivated chiefly for feeding horses. . . . About Woodbridge, they have been in the habit of selling the greatest part of their crops for the London markets." Potatoes: "This root has not been cultivated in Suffolk till within a few years . . . in general they are not much attended to; not so much as they ought to be by cottagers."

Hemp:

The district of country in which this article of cultivation is chiefly found, extends from Eye to Beccles. . . . The soil preferred, is, what is called in the district, mixed land, that is, sandy loam, moist and putrid, but without being stiff or tenacious. . . . No weeding is ever given to it, the hemp destroying every other plant. . . . It is tied up in small bundles called baits. . . . It is always water retted.

Exceeding good huckabacks is also made from hemp, for towels and common table cloths. The low priced hemps are a general wear for husbandmen, servants, and labouring manufacturers; the sorts from 18d to 2s. per yard, are the usual wear of farmers and tradesmen; the finer sorts . . . are preferred by many gentlemen, for strength and warmth, to other linen.

Grass: "Suffolk is not famous for its grass lands, either in respect of fertility or management. Haymaking is but imperfectly practised, the grass is left too long after the scythe, nor is there sufficient attention to grass cocks and those of second size. Too much is left to the hazard of weather; nor is there sufficient care taken to tread the stacks enough in making; they are rarely pulled, but left loose and rough on the surface and the practice of trussing is but now coming slowly in."

In his chapter on gardens and orchards comes the first mention of those crinkle-crankle walls, to be found round old Suffolk gardens. "I have only to observe one practice, not common elsewhere, which is, that building garden walls, no more than the breadth of a common brick in thickness, by means of waving the line. The saving is considerable. In regard to the effect, both in point of duration and fruit, accounts are various; and the introduction of this method is not of sufficient date to ascertain it satisfactorily."

Cattle: "The cows of Suffolk have long been celebrated for their great quantity of milk, which, I believe, much exceeds, on an average, that of any other breed in the island, if quantity of food and size of the animal are taken into the account. . . . The breed is universally polled . . . the size small; few rise when fattened, to above 50 stone."

Agricultural societies: "The only society of this sort ever established in Suffolk, is the present existing one, called the Melford Society, which now meets alternatively at Bury and Melford."

This book was reprinted in 1969.

The result of all this sowing would be the harvest, which Tusser managed to divide into ten parts:

1 One part cast forth, for rent due out of hand.
2 One other part, for seed to sow thy land.
3 Another part, leave parson for his tithe.

4 Another part for harvest sickle and scythe.
5 One part for plough-wright, cart-wright, knacker and smith.
6 One part, to uphold thy team that draw therewith.
7 One part, for servant, and workman's wages lay.
8 One part, likewise, for fill-belly, day by day.
9 One part thy wife, for needful things doth crave.
10 Thyself and child, the last one part would have.

There were certain common lands accessible to villagers, such as about forty acres, lying open to the beach, at Walberswick. "All persons resident in the parish and belonging thereto, have a right to turn on any quantity of stock they may choose, at all times. Some of the farmers in consequence turn on from ten to twelve head of stock, each. Several of the poor feed it with a great many geese, but a large number do not derive any benefit from it. This marsh land is liable to be inundated by extraordinary high tides, there not being any wall to protect it."

When each county evolved its own wagon, with colours peculiar to itself, Suffolk was not backward. But no other county could lay claim to an hermaphrodite wagon (in local parlance a 'morphadite'). This consisted of a tumbrel, the shafts of which were fastened to a forward extension also with shafts, thus providing a double loading platform most useful in haysel (hay-making) and harvest. When not required for such purposes, the tumbrel could be detached and used in the ordinary way.

In 1868 Mr. James Duncan, a merchant of Mincing Lane, determined to try to establish some method of encouraging the English cultivation of the beet root, and of making sugar from it. Unfortunately this failed through lack of support from the farmers, who knew nothing of the crop needed and because of rather primitive equipment and a lack of knowledge of sugar chemistry. They even ran into difficulties over the disposal of the effluent. Two old sugar-loaf containers, used from 1868 to 1874, are to be found in the Lavenham Museum.

The home sugar enterprise went through hard times until the passing of the Sugar Industry (Subsidy) Act of 1925, which marked the beginning of the industry and created a new era in farming. It has become an all-important cash and cleaning crop. The drudgery of this harvesting has been removed by the sugar beet harvester.

A survey of the agriculture of Suffolk, published by Mr. P. J. O. Trist in 1969, must rank for modern farming with Arthur Young's survey. Yet methods and conditions are changing so fast that, as it took four years to make this really remarkable and comprehensive work on Suffolk farming, some of it would appear to be out of date.

Many of the small farms that have been bought up in recent years are no longer recognizable, because field boundaries have gone, and in some cases the farmhouse has been destroyed. Since the mid-1950s, the introduction of the combine harvester, and the need to reduce costs of cultivation have necessitated the amalgamation of fields. This has led to the grubbing-up of the hedgerows and the filling-in of ditches; which in turn has abolished hedging, ditching, and dung carting and spreading. The depression of the 1930s left many farm buildings in a derelict condition, and modern farm machinery has made them redundant.

When the figures for combine harvesters as given by Mr. Trist are considered—such as 32 in use in 1942 and 2,970 in 1968—one realizes how the old methods have disappeared, such as stooking, carting, stacking, thatching, with thrashing as the great climax. Stacks of corn neatly thatched are no longer to be seen. The stack-yard of the old farming system was always such a lovely sight, the visible result of a great and satisfying achievement. Yet this mechanization with heavy machinery is creating difficulties on some land. But the demand for land of any kind in Suffolk is intense. To the credit of scientific methods, large areas of heath-land have been brought under cultivation.

All kinds of new crops have appeared. The vining pea crop is very significant, and other vegetables grown for the quick-freeze industry. Suffolk also grows the largest acreage of asparagus in the country.

More cattle have been kept indoors and fed on the barley beef system. Prior to 1939 the rearing and fattening of turkeys in Suffolk was a relatively small business, but this has grown enormously, as figures supplied by Trist show—1930, 48,733 birds, which by 1968 had become 367,696. Then Suffolk has the largest pig population of any county in England and Wales. I was also very interested to note the 1,000 acres of Suffolk Fen, owned by Bryant and May, are planted with poplars for matches. (When I go to town I always note their factory, just three miles from London.)

Yet amid all this change, old customs still prevail. Marsh grazing that was let by auction for a year or period of years, is still so let. This applies to those at Aldeburgh, Southwold and Beccles Corporation Marshes, on the Waveney level at Bungay, and between Beccles and Oulton.

The East Suffolk Sea Flood of 1953 inundated many of these, because 20,000 out of a total of 24,000 acres of Suffolk marshes were covered with eight or nine feet of salt water. This called forth a certain amount of heroism. At Holm Hill, Felixstowe, two horses were rescued by Alfred Adams and his nephew David Adams. At Kirton, after several men had given up hope of rescuing horses in deep water in a barn, Alfred Adams rode into the barn alone and encouraged them to come out and cross the marsh to safety.

It is rather remarkable that one county has produced three separate breeds of animals it can call its own: the Suffolk Punch, the red poll cattle and the Suffolk sheep; to say nothing of black pigs. But these latter have been found also in Cornwall.

The black-faced sheep were evolved early in the nineteenth century by crossing the old Norfolk horned ewes (now almost extinct) with the Southdown rams. From 1800 to 1850 this inter-breeding was very general. In their essay on the agriculture of Suffolk, William and Hugh Raynbird of Hengrave, in 1847, said: "Breeding sheep are chiefly a cross between the Down and Old Norfolk. It is in the breed of sheep that the greatest improvement has taken place. The restless Norfolk is now rarely seen, their place being taken by the Southdown, or by a cross between that breed and the old Norfolk—a breed equally hardy, with greater fattening properties than the old Norfolk."

> Old Norfolks will serve well enough
> To dung our sands unless indeed
> They prove that some outlandish breed
> Are hardier and can further ramble
> To pick scant food or nimble scramble

With stray bare legs and bellies high
Through brake, broom, furze, heath, wet or dry.

1808

By the middle of the century these Southdown-Norfolks were widely known as 'black-faces' and in 1859 were christened 'Suffolks', classes being provided for them at the Suffolk Agricultural Association Meetings.

The Suffolk Sheep Society was established in the spring of 1886, for the purpose of promoting the purity of the breed and providing a reliable guarantee to buyers by maintaining a register of pure-bred sires. A flock prize competition instituted by the society secured a sufficient number of entries the first year to prove that it was appreciated by the breeders.

In the first *Flock Book* the following points in which they excelled were given. Fecundity: thirty lambs reared per score of ewes is a frequent average. Early maturity: if well grazed they are fit for the butcher at ten or twelve months old, and the ram lambs are so forward at seven or eight months that they are preferred as tups to older sheep by nineteen breeders out of twenty.

Hardihood: they will get a living and thrive where other breeds would starve. Mutton: the quality is super-excellent, with an exceptionally larger proportion of lean meat, and commands a ready sale at top price. Constitution: their robust, hardy character, power of endurance, and comparative freedom from attacks of foot-rot, have during the past ten years caused them to displace to a large extent the half-bred sheep formerly in favour in marshland districts.

Then follow the agreed scale of points for judges:

Head—Hornless, Face black and long, and Muzzle moderately fine, especially in ewes. (A small quantity of clean white wool on the forehead not objected to.) Ears a medium length, black, and fine texture. Eyes bright and full. 25.

Neck—Moderate length and well set (in rams stronger, with good crest). 5.

Shoulder—Broad and oblique. 5.

Chest—Deep and wide. 5.

Back and Loin—Long, level, and well covered with meat and muscle; tail broad and well set up. The ribs long and well sprung, with a full flank. 20.

Legs and Feet—Straight and black, with flat bone, fine and of good quality. Wooled to knees and hocks, clean below, fore-legs set well apart, hind legs well filled with mutton. 20.

Belly—Well covered with wool (Also scrotum of rams). 5.

Fleece—Moderately short; close with lustrous fibre, without tendency to mat or felt together, and well defined, i.e. not shading into dark wool or hair. 10.

Skin—Fine, soft and pink colour. 5. = 100.

The Suffolks were extensively used in cross-breeding, partly because of the absence of wool on the face and the legs. This clean-headed character has made them popular for mating with other breeds of a smaller size. They can claim to be the most widely distributed of all the Down breeds.

There were some eminent breeders in those days, as also some eminent shepherds. Such, for example, was Ishmael Cutter, shepherd to the Earl of Stradbroke. In 1833 he reared 566 lambs from 406 ewes; in 1834 717 lambs from 487 ewes with a loss of 17 ewes; in 1837 606 lambs from 413 ewes, with a loss of 6 ewes. In 1835, it was resolved by the Agricultural Association "That Ishmael Cutter be presented with the Honorary Silver Medal, as an acknowledgement of the high services entertained by the Committee, for having reared more lambs from a given number of ewes than any other Shepherd within the limits of this Association during the past four years." Ishmael continued to win prizes for a number of years after this.

Then in 1853, James Meadows of Iken reared 636 lambs from 410 ewes, with a loss of only 6 ewes (31 lambs to the score), and at the same time Henry Cooper reared 392 lambs from 240 ewes, with a loss of only 3 ewes (32 lambs to the score). These were remarkable performances, especially in those days when there was no artificial feeding.

Ishmael's name reminds one of the eccentric old lady, somewhere in these parts, who had thirty or forty sheep, that would follow her about like dogs. She had given them all biblical names, such as Nathan, David, Solomon, Peter, and they would answer to her call. Once upon a time the smell of sheep was considered a cure for whooping cough.

In 1858 at Bury St. Edmunds prizes of £5 and £2 were given for the best pen of five black-faced shearling ewes. George

Dobito came first, and Wm. Wilson second. This was the first appearance of the breed in the Suffolk Show catalogues; and for many years afterwards they were described as the black-faced breed, now named 'The Suffolk'.

In 1931 it was said: "They have, of course, immensely improved and now stand second to none in England." An American Suffolk Sheep Society was started in 1930. They were increasing in demand in South Africa, Canada and Australia. Coming down the years, 1969 was a record year for the export of these sheep, when 1,230 animals went to twelve countries. France topped the list by taking 886. Then in April 1970, 96 Suffolk sheep were exported to Hungary, the second batch to be sold to them in just over two months. Now in these days comes the news that the Suffolks have figured in the Paris Show on the British Stand, and that lamb cutlets, with redcurrant jelly and mint sauce, with French roll and cider, are likely to appear on the French menus.

At the Royal Show of 1867, held at Bury St. Edmunds, this comment was made by a steward: "The Black-faced Suffolk must possess qualities which a stranger knows not of. The men of Norfolk and Suffolk know their business too well to make it safe to assume that their sheep are as bad as they look, and there must be some merit, though not visible, to compensate for all their faults. Still, it seems difficult to understand their good qualities, whatever they are, might not be retained with some modification at least of the long legs, short ribs, thin neck, bare backs and naked heads that characterize the Suffolk sheep shown at Bury."

But at Preston in 1885, this is what they said: ". . . a variety of much merit as should now be recognized by a separate class, combining as they do so large a quantity of mutton of fine quality with a fleece of more than medium weight, and being also extremely valuable for the purpose of cross breeding."

1966 saw the last of the folded flocks on the heavy land of East Suffolk. In the old days the shepherd would turn them out of the folds about ten o'clock and a boy would take them off to the heath, while the shepherd would prepare the folds for the evening return.

Lambing was always hard work with many sleepless nights. In the old days the shepherd was allowed a bottle of whisky and a cask of ale for the period. And his cries would have reached

Timber-framed barn, typical outbuilding of the Suffolk farmyard

heaven if they had not been forthcoming. Then, in shearing, he worked for the result and not for speed. They even had a name for certain weather, because they called the storms that happen about the time that lambs fall 'lamb-storms'.

At the Royal Show in 1971, Seisdon Royal, an outstanding shearling ram, bred and exhibited by Mr. John Farquarson, won first prize in the breed class for shearling rams and then went on to win the experimental inter-breed competition with a convincing 214 points, with Hampshire entry 207 and the Dorset Down 169.

A ram lamb from the Lawshall flock of W. G. Waspe and Son, of Bury St. Edmunds, sold for 1,000 guineas at the Suffolk Sheep Society's annual show and sale at Ipswich in 1972. But in 1964, when the sale was on the Suffolk Showground, a ram lamb sold for 1,100 guineas.*

Crabbe described his county sheep in none too flattering terms, as usual:

> The Lover rode as hasty riders ride,
> And reached a common pasture wild and wide:
> Small black legged sheep devour with hunger keen
> The meagre herbage, fleshless, lank and lean:
> Such o'er thy level turf Newmarket! stray,
> And there with other blacklegs find their prey.

The story of cattle is as old as history, but the records of herds, or breeds, is quite another matter. As far as Suffolk is concerned polled cattle had long existed before Arthur Young made his survey. Before that John Kirby had noted them in his *Suffolk Traveller* of 1732–4, and spoke of the butter produced from them as being "justly esteemed the pleasantest and best in England". Their Suffolk grounds was a tract of country 25 miles by 12, from Coddenham to Bruisyard and from Brome to Gipping. His description was: "The breed is universally polled, that is without horns, the size small . . . a clean throat, with little dewlap; a snake's head; clean thin legs and short; a springing rib and a large carcase; a flat loin, the hip bones to lie square and even; the tail to rise high from the rump."

He goes on: "The greatest fault with their management is the

* 1,000 guineas was £1,150; 1,100 guineas was £1,155.

carelessness with which they breed. There is no such thing in the county as a bull more than three years old; two years the common age. The consequence of this is inevitably that before the merit can be known of the stock gotten, the bull is no more. It must be obvious that such a system precludes all improvements. It springs very much from the want of the spirit of breeding getting into this country." Many of the old Suffolk polled cattle were much more massive beasts than the Norfolk and could be easily picked out by the coarseness of the head.

This was really a description of the old Suffolk dun cow. Afterwards a deep, rich blood-red was considered a mark of excellence.

A better state of affairs did not exist until the rise of the agricultural societies, which in Suffolk commenced in 1831. Even the breeders like the Earl of Stradbroke and Sir E. Kerrison announced that as far as they were concerned, colour did not matter. However, Mr. W. Biddell of Playford thought differently; he said, "We have got the Suffolk cows into a first-class breed, and red is the colour, and we had better stick to it. They have become an established breed, so red and so like, that they always produce a like progeny, showing that they are not a cross bred." Again: "I recollect the time when no other colour than red in a Suffolk cow would be looked at."

Suffolk red polled stock had been bred for a long time by Messrs. Biddell. The animals had been carefully selected for their milking and early fattening properties. The Biddells were for a long time in advance of other Suffolk breeders in their preference for good red, whole-coloured animals as representing the purest blood of the Suffolk polled stocks.

The year 1846 saw the amalgamation of the Norfolk and Suffolk varieties and they were then known as red polled cattle. This was later altered to red poll in 1909. Mention might be made at this point of the subtle difference between the terms polled and poll. The first suggests that the beasts had been artificially polled instead of being native born polled cattle. Now follows the official description.

"Colour—Red. The tip of the tail, and the udder may be white. The extension of the white of the udder a few inches along the inside of the flank, or a small white spot or mark on the under part of the belly by the milk veins, shall not be held to disqualify an animal whose sire and dam form part of an established herd of the breed, or answer all the essentials of this 'Standard Description'.

"Form—There should be no horns, slugs, or abortive horns." (Slugs, be it noted, were horny substances adhering to the skin over the seat of natural horns, free from any attachment to the skull but more or less undeveloped as horns.)

Points of superior animals were "a deep red colour, with udder of the same colour, but the tip of the tail may be white. Nose not dark or cloudy. Form—A neat head and throat. A full eye. A tuft or crest of hair should hang over the forehead. The frontal bones should begin to contract a little above the eyes and should terminate in a comparatively narrow prominence at the summit of the head."

The *Herd Book* was established in 1883 under the editorship of H. F. Euren. He had previously issued a *Foundation Volume* in 1877 on his own account. But the title Norfolk and Suffolk was never accepted by Suffolk, who insisted on being called the Suffolk Society. It was not until 1888 that the "Red Poll Society" was formed and purchased Mr. Euren's copyright and adopted his previous volume. He, however, remained secretary until 1895.

The advantages of hornless cattle were several. They were docile as cows, and this recommended them as park cattle; also it was of no little gain when horses came into the pasture, or when stock was sent to market and had to make long railway journeys. Also the deep red harmonized well with the landscape.

But some will say why all this concern about colour and breed? First, the red polls were found to lay on flesh rapidly on pasture of the poorest character, where other breeds needed an additional supply. Then they were good milkers. It was found that three quarts milk gave two and a third ounces of cream more than that of the Longhorns, which were then popular, after standing thirty-six hours, and churned one-fourth more butter.

Then again, they proved to be dual-purpose animals, and the aim of the society has been to perpetuate and continually improve the animals that will give a consistently high average yield of high-class milk, and from which steers can be reared to provide prime carcases of beef. The highest yields have not been sought after, though herds of over 1,000 gallons average are common, and 2,000-gallon cows have not been unknown. With constitution come regular breeding and a calf every year, or at most every fourteen months. Outstanding features are:

1. Long lactation.
2. Longevity and regularity of breeding.
3. Hardy constitution and low cost of feeding.
4. The lowest percentage of herd replacement.
5. Early maturity of prime beef production.

One writer has summed it all up: "It may be a small point in this utilitarian age, but is there a more beautiful sight to the cattle lover than a matched herd of these blood-red beauties swishing their white tails as they contentedly graze."

At the Royal Show in 1851, held at Windsor, in the class for Welsh, Irish and other pure breeds, all the awards went to the red polls, still shown under the old names of the Suffolk and Norfolk polled.

Sadly, these famous red polls are on the wane, their places being taken by the Friesians. Yet they are still famous in countries like Australia, and have flourished in Columbia, Uganda and Zambia.

We might end with an account of the terrible disease of cattle plague that broke out in 1868. It appears that a ship called the *Joseph Soames* left Cronstadt* on 16th July 1866 with fifty-eight cattle on board destined for Hull, where they arrived on 25th July. After the animals had been examined by the veterinary inspector, he reported that some of them were suffering from cattle plague. Under the circumstances it was decided that the whole cargo should be slaughtered and the carcases destroyed. But a serious difficulty arose, because no ground was available where the carcases could be buried, without taking them through the streets of the town, and no appliances existed for the destruction by burning or boiling. The only course seemed to be to sink them at sea. Ships were taken to carry them out. The carcases were packed in two lighters, battened down, roped across and towed out. But the means taken to sink the lighters were quite inadequate, and nearly all the carcases were cast ashore on various parts of the Lincolnshire and Norfolk coast, and the disease spread wholesale. It was stated that cattle plague had a close affinity to

* Cronstadt: now Kronshtadt. It is an island port near Leningrad.

typhoid fever and smallpox in human beings. The inspectors appointed seemed quite unfit for their duties; they carried the disease wherever they went, and often left it where they did not find it. No compensation being paid for slaughter, the owners felt no compunction in clearing off the greater portion of their stocks before hoisting the blue flag.

This awful calamity slowly died out, but not before causing ruin to hundreds of farmers through the length and breadth of the land. Most fortunately sheep were rarely affected, and swine seemed quite immune.

The Suffolk red polls have been always a great feature at the Suffolk shows, except when plague has prevented their appearance.

The chestnut horse was probably an indigenous type, but it was perfected by an old Suffolk farmer, Thomas Crisp of Ufford, in the late eighteenth century. In 1773 he advertised his unnamed chestnut horse "to get a good stock for coach or road"; and from this horse nearly every Suffolk Punch is descended. In a later generation his grandson, another Thomas Crisp, building upon the foundation laid by his forbear, moved from Rendlesham to Butley Abbey and there won international fame as a breeder, not merely of the Punch but of prize-winning shorthorn cattle and of black Suffolk, small white and Berkshire pigs.

The two great authorities on the Suffolk horse are Sir John Cullum, writing in his *History of Hawstead* in 1724, and Arthur Young in his general survey. Moreover, the first *Suffolk Stud Book* is dedicated to this splendid animal. It is a bulky volume, as big as a family Bible, and contrasts strangely with the slim little book published in 1960.

The chief fault of the Suffolk horse was defective feet. These were inclined to be pinched at the heels and shallow over the bars. The horn also was of poor quality, being rather brittle. However, a good deal of attention has been paid to this, and feet classes are still held by the society at its shows.

This is what Cullum had to say:

Having mentioned horses, I must take this opportunity of doing justice to a most useful breed of that noble animal, not indeed peculiar to this parish, but, I believe, to the county. This breed is well known by the name of Suffolk Punches. They are generally about 15 hands high, of remarkably short and compact make; their legs bony; and their shoulders loaded with flesh. (The first Thomas Crisp's horse was 15½ hands.) Their colour is often of a light sorrel, which is much remarked in some distinct parts of the kingdom, as their form. They are not made to indulge the rapid impatience of this posting generation; but, for draught, they are perhaps unrivalled, as for their gentle and tractable temper; and to exhibit proofs of their great powers, drawing matches are sometimes made; and the proprietors are as anxious for the success of their respective horses, as those can be, whose racers aspire to the plates at Newmarket. . . . But truth obliges me to add, though not to the credit of my compatriots, that those creatures, formed so well by nature, are almost always disfigured by art. Because their long tails might, in dirty seasons, be something inconvenient, they are therefore cut off frequently to within four inches of the rump, so that they scarcely afford hold for a crupper; and as absurdity never knows where to stop, even the poor remaining stump has frequently half its hair clipped off. In a provincial paper, a few years ago, one of these mutilated animals was expressively described, as having a shorn mane, and a very short bung'd dock.

This is what Arthur Young had to say:

The Suffolk breed of horses, is no less celebrated than the cows. They are found in most perfection in the district of country that is upon the coast extending to Woodbridge, Debenham, Eye and Lowestoft. The best of all were found some years ago upon the Sandlings, south of Woodbridge and Orford. Amongst the great farmers in that country, there was, forty years ago, a considerable spirit of breeding, and of drawing team against team for large sums of money. Mr Mays of Ramsholt dock, was said to have drawn fifteen horses for 1500 guineas.* It is regretted that such a spirit of emulation was lost.—I remember seeing many of the old breed, which were very famous, and, in some respects, an uglier horse could not be viewed; sorrel colour, very low in the fore-end, a large ill-shaped head, with slouching heavy ears, a great carcase and short legs, but short backed, and more of the punch than the Leicestershire breeders will allow. These horses could only walk and draw; they could trot no better than a cow. But their power in drawing was very considerable. Of late years, by aiming at Coach-horses, the breed is much changed to a handsome, lighter, and more active

* 1,500 guineas was £1,575.

horse. It is yet an excellent breed. . . . Of all branches of live stock, perhaps nothing is in such an imperfect state as working oxen, in most things that concern them, we are in an infancy of agriculture.

Another authority, William Youatt, 1847, said: "The excellence, and a rare one, of the old Suffolk [horse] consisted in nimbleness of action, and the honesty and continuation with which he would exert himself at a dead pull. Many a good draught horse knows well what he can effect; and after he has attempted it and failed, no torture of the whip can induce him to strain his powers beyond their natural extent. The Suffolk, however, would tug at a dead pull until he drops. It was beautiful to see a team of true Suffolks, at a signal from the driver, and without whip, down on their knees in a moment and drag everything before them."

Naturally, horses of such a description caused a race of grooms to spring up who loved these beautiful creatures and could find no fault in them. Such a one was old Joseph Pattle, who looked after a horse that was blind. "Yes, sir, he was as blind as a bat of both eyes, and no one ever found it out but a boy. When we came along the road, the little rascal sang out—'Master, your horse is blind!' 'Go away,' said I, 'he's all right.' He saw me chuck the bridle when we came to stones."

Then there was the one who took a pair to Windsor in 1851, and they won first and second prizes under the very eyes of Queen Victoria. "Trot on, my man," said one of the judges. "Run on, you with No. 407." "What d'ye want to trot him for?" came the reply. "Why, you mayn't run such horses as these." However, the old groom thought the castle grounds were a "proper nice place", but he wondered the Queen let the unclothed statuary—"sich things as them be in her garden".

The Suffolk horse is not yet extinct. One breeder that I know travels three stallions a year, and twelve new members have joined the society recently. Small farms with well-to-do owners are using them instead of tractors, but there is a shortage of utensils fit for their use.

In 1867 the Royal Show visited Suffolk for the first time. There was a great rivalry between Ipswich and Bury for the honour of entertaining it, and Bury won. One small boy at the time remembered the excitement of the occasion, as it was his first excursion by train. He said: "We travelled in open carriages, and having swallowed pints of dust and yards of smoke, arrived safely at our destination, and I had the satisfaction of seeing my grandfather's mare, 'Royal Moggy', win the first prize of £20."

This is what was said at the Centenary Show in 1939: "The breeding class for Draught Horses were generally good, with the Suffolks, as has commonly happened in recent years, providing the highest entry. The outstanding feature of the section was, however, the display of four-horse teams in harness. Here, again, the Suffolk was most largely represented, though many house-wives thought the first-prize Shire team, of four really magnificent greys, was the most remarkable of all. On the other hand, it was one of the Suffolk teams, parading in old-time harness with its full complement of brasses and bells, which was the favourite with the ringside crowd."

At the Royal Show of 1960 there were 265 entries, more than double the number of any other breed in the heavy horse section. One of the highlights was undoubtedly the parade of Suffolk horses only in the Grand Ring on the second day.

It has been said often that Suffolk horses look at their best when the sun shines on their all chestnut colour. One of the presidents remarked that Suffolk people are like the Punches, when they put their shoulder to the collar, something has got to move. It might be mentioned that there was a Suffolk horse stud at Sandringham, established during the reign of King George VI. 1961 saw the last of the famous stallion shows held at Ipswich.

Just as the horse was at the basis of all warlike activities, from feudal times, kept and maintained by the knights; so the Suffolk Punch achieved fame and a waning glory in the First World War, in handling and hauling the great guns which its immense strength enabled it to do. It was so soon to be superseded by the internal combustion engine.

It is a curious fact that the first Suffolk Show commenced on the eastern side of the county, and did not include the western half. This was the East Suffolk Association, which had its birth as long ago as 1831. Two years later this was followed by the West Suffolk Association which was also followed in turn by the South Suffolk Societies in 1835, and the Central Suffolk Association with headquarters at Stowmarket in 1840. There were also at this time a number of farmers' clubs founded, including the Ashbocking Club in 1837, proudly claiming to be the first such club in England and the one from which all the others took their rules. Between 1837 and 1840 these clubs were established at Beccles, Debenham, Framlingham, Hadleigh, Halesworth, Needham Market, Sudbury, Wickham Market, Wrentham, Woodbridge and Yoxford. It must be realized that Suffolk then was essentially rural, though somewhat divided on agricultural policy. It was not until 1856 that the Suffolk Agricultural Association united the county into one.

Prior to 1831 annual shows of sheep and lambs were held, several dealers and 'growers' combining for this purpose. The first show of the East Suffolk Association, which grew out of the annual small shows, was held at Wickham Market on Friday, 21st September 1832, when the following prizes were offered: £10 for horses, £10 for cattle, £20 for sheep and £2 for pigs, £12 to men for long service, £8 to female dairy servants, £7 to shepherds rearing the most lambs and £14 for the best ploughmen. The large sum of 10s. was awarded to Samuel Richardson of Ramsholt for his hand corn-threshing machine. The comment by the *Ipswich Journal* on the event was: "The exhibition of stock was anything but great, yet what was shown was of superior quality." Mr. J. Mosely of Glemham House and Lord Huntingfield were the principal exhibitors, but both refused to take the awards made to them. This procedure was followed by other winners for some years.

Lord Stradbroke was the first president, an office he occupied until 1865, after which he was elected patron, a position he kept until his death in 1886. He had served in the Peninsular War, receiving a medal with five clasps. It was said of him that he was beloved and respected by the whole county.

Mention might be made of the first secretary, Mr Cornelius Welton, who was born at Wilby in 1801. His brother was the Reverend Dr. Welton, a pioneer of medical missions in China. Cornelius was a remarkable man, who had an extensive business as a land agent and valuer. He was also an enthusiastic volunteer with the rank of lieutenant. He was one of the founders of Framlingham College, being its first secretary.

From 1832 to 1834, shows were held alternately at Wickham Market and Saxmundham, in the month of September. After that various towns provided accommodation, such as Halesworth in 1845, Woodbridge in 1846, Framlingham in 1847.

The occasion when the show was held at Christchurch Park, Ipswich, in 1839, inspired John Duval (1816–92) with one of his best pictures. He illustrated the first *Suffolk Stud Book*. The principal figures in the painting were all local worthies and he has included himself lounging on the grass. This now hangs in the picture gallery at Ipswich Museum.

Some of the events that took place in its years of history make interesting reading. For instance, there was a show dinner at Beccles in 1871, given by the judges, stewards and members of the local committees. This started at seven o'clock in the evening and lasted until 2 a.m. the next morning. Needless to say a lot of wine was consumed. When the bill came in several members who had not been fortunate enough to be invited protested loudly, and said that something must be done. But the difficulty was to know what. It was therefore necessary to find a scapegoat, so it was decided to go for mine host at the 'King's Head'. The committee's point was that the bill was excessive and that it was quite impossible for so much wine to have been consumed. The judge, however, thought otherwise, and in summing up, said: "It is wonderful how wine goes down when it hasn't to be paid for, and there must be a little licence on the occasion of a Show. They must not be too particular for a bottle or two, and considering the importance of the event and the length of the dinner, he did not think a bottle and a half per man a bit too much"; and gave judgement accordingly. Besides, the landlord had kept a very good record.

At the Wickham Market Show on 20th September 1838, it was reported: "At 4 o'clock, 390 gentlemen partook of an elegant entertainment provided by Mr. Tyce, of the White Hart, in a large building, which had been fitted up for the purpose." At this function the Earl of Stradbroke made this remarkable statement that "he was looking forward to the time when they should plough without horses and sow and reap at half the present expense". Sir Thomas Gooch said: "The country wants an administration that will go heart and hand with the agricultural interests. The manufacturers are all in a flourishing condition, while we poor devils are ground to the dust."

Prizes for all sorts of things were offered. For example in 1840 William Long of Hurts Hall, Saxmundham, offered a premium of five guineas for the best geological essay on the nature and properties of the soil and substratum in East Suffolk. This was a bit too much for most, who rather shied at such a subject. However, a Captain H. Alexander had a go, and brought the subject to a close with Noah's Flood.

A prize was also offered to the labourers in husbandry, whose rent did not exceed £5 a year, and by whom the greatest number of legitimate children had been brought up to the age of 6 years, with or without the least parochial relief. When the show was at Framlingham in 1860, fifteen men were awarded prizes, and their families averaged a little over twelve children each. One man mustered eighteen, his rent being £4 and relief given in sickness only amounted to £5 17s. Another had twelve children, his rent being £3 10s. and the only relief that he had received was "Mutton and Porter" during his wife's confinements.

For the first 30 years there was no attempt to house the animals, the horses and cattle being simply held by horsemen and stockmen at equidistant stakes, which were driven into the ground. But in 1858 a resolution was passed that £100 of the funds be placed to a deposit account with the intention of appropriating it to the erection of sheds. In 1861 the stewards were empowered to erect temporary coverings for the sheep and pigs, to protect them from heat or rain, the expense not to exceed £10.

In 1869 the two-day shows commenced, and the growth of attendance rose from 3,367 in 1857 to 28,027 in 1902. In 1861 implements were first exhibited at Ipswich. Innovations were recorded at the Stowmarket Show of 1890 when dairy competitions were introduced; and the implement field trials were restarted, after a lapse of some years, at the same place in 1903. Sheep-shearing and horse-shoeing competitions were also held. Sheep dog trials was the attraction in 1906, in which wild mountain sheep were used. Also competitions in poultry trussing were inaugurated. It was said of the 1906 show that exhibits of implements had increased every year, and was one of the most important sections of the show.

In 1850 Richard Garrett of Leiston Works offered prizes to the servant who took the best care of and kept in the best order his master's machinery.

The centenary show was held at Ipswich in June 1931, under the presidency of the Right Hon. E. G. Pretyman. This attracted many strangers from a distance who were greatly impressed with the remarkable displays representing the three breeds of Suffolk, each of which was large enough to make separate exhibitions. The president carried all with him when he emphasized at the luncheon that one of agriculture's greatest assets lay in its human touch. He scored a great success with a Suffolk mare and a red poll cow. A spectacle very much to the taste of the crowd was the entry into the ring of three teams of four grand Suffolk horses, drawing huge farm wagons. The president's team were drawing a loaded wagon covered by a sheet on which was painted 1831 and 1931. The horses were accompanied by drivers attired in old-time smocks, quilted and embossed.

Farming was then in the doldrums, but this is what Lord Stradbroke (the son of the first president) said at the luncheon. "He hoped that young men would not lose heart and keep out of farming, and he also hoped that when the time came for them to marry they would choose wives who would be willing to live in the country. He hoped they would be as fortunate as himself and the President had been."

The show obtained a permanent ground at Bucklesham Road, Ipswich, by 1960, when it held its exhibition that year. It has just been suggested that these quite beautiful grounds, ideal for the purpose for which they were acquired, should be available as a leisure park. An old-time farmyard is to be constructed and—what is particularly encouraging—older breeds as well as modern stock are to be encouraged and preserved.

The Towns

He gives direction to the town,
To cry it up, or run it down.

Swift

One of the criticisms of the county made by outsiders and those anxious to dispose of their wares, was that it had but few towns. However the two capitals at once spring to the mind, that of Ipswich and Bury St. Edmunds, both dominated by one figure; Bury by the kingly martyr St. Edmund, and the other by Cardinal Wolsey. But, of course, there are the various little market towns dotted about, such as Woodbridge, Framlingham, Stowmarket, Needham, Sudbury, Beccles and Bungay. Each as individual as they could be until modern architects and developers have set to work to make them alike into a characterless exactness peculiar to our faceless age. Let us then begin with Ipswich.

As one looks down on the city one is tempted to remark, can anything good come out of Ipswich? Once upon a time it called forth fair remarks and nostalgic memories, because another Ipswich sprang up in Massachusetts, founded by twelve good men who rowed up their river from Boston and founded a delightful little township and gave it a name they loved, because it reminded them of home. They even managed to get a coaching clock, made by George Moore of the Suffolk Ipswich, to put in their prettily situated, white-painted North Church—now, alas, destroyed by lightning.

It is curious how history repeats itself. Once upon a time the Suffolk town was famous for the manufacture of broadcloth and other woollens. Then this died out and the population declined, with the result there were empty houses and Ipswich became known as a town without people. Just think of it! But the tide

The Thoroughfare, Ipswich

turned and then comes the statement that it was difficult to procure a house that would accommodate a middling family, "all such being in a manner scrambled for".

Needless to say it has always been a market town. Tuesdays and Thursdays were for butchers' meat, Wednesdays and Fridays for fish (stale, from local reports because the fishermen were too lazy to fish in local waters), and Saturday was a general sort of affair for all kinds of things.

One character stands out above all others—it was a town good to its children. There was, of course, the famous grammar school founded by Edward VI, but there were no less than five charity schools for poor children. One was Christ's Hospital for twenty blue-coat boys, who were found in everything, clothes, meat, drink, washing, lodging; and taught to read, made to work, then bound out to sea. There was another for sixteen red-sleeved boys, another for sixty grey-coat boys. Then comes one for twenty-four blue-coat girls, who were taught to read, to knit, to sew, and fitted out for service. And finally one for sixteen green-sleeved boys, supported by the Dissenters. It must have been rather funny to see this kind of harlequinade amongst the boys and girls.

In the year 1663 comes this court order: "For the better preservation of the children which are walking or playing in the common streets of this town, that every person coming with cart or tumbrel, shall, for the time coming, leading the horse of such team in such manner that one wheel may roll on the one side of the channel, and the other on the other side [ruts in the road]: and such as offend therin shall forfeit 12d. for the use of the poor. And no person shall ride upon any cart or tumbril in this town, under pain of forfeiting 12d. for each offence."

When Waterloo was won, a general illumination took place, at the expense of the Society of Friends; an excellent dinner of roast and boiled beef was given to all the poor children of the different schools. The tables were set out in the new market place, which was decorated with flowers and shrubs. What a burble they must have made.

At the end of 1693 fifty families of French Protestants who manufactured lutestrings were admitted to the town, and "they shall have £20 a year, for two years; and they shall not be rated nor put into any office for seven years".

On 3rd July 1772 fourteen horses were entered for the races and every day the heats were most severely contested. Owing to the influence of Sir Charles Bunbury, Ipswich races at this period were attended by a great concourse of persons of fashion and excited great interest in the sporting world.

December 1778 saw a scuffle with the press-gang and a party of men at the 'Green Man'. Mr. Thomas Nichols, master of the Ram Inn ventured to interfere and was so badly hurt that he died the next morning. Two midshipmen and fifteen men were tried for this, but acquitted.

In 1793 an Act of Parliament was obtained for paving, lighting, cleansing and otherwise improving the town of Ipswich. On Monday, 5th August, the first stone of the new pavement was laid at the Bell corner near the Cornhill. Then on 17th August this same year, the body of Lieutenant Lionel Tollemache, the last male heir of this ancient family, passed through the town. He was killed by a shell at Valenciennes.

In January 1795, in consequence of a rapid thaw and the frost returning, several persons were seen skating through the principal streets of the town. On 6th July 1800 Lord Nelson was chosen high steward of the borough in the place of Lionel Tollemache.

In May 1724 comes this entry: "The Ipswich Spaw Waters is now owned by Mrs. Martha Coward, and Attendance will be given every morning at the Bath on St. Margaret's Green, from 6 to 9 at One Penny per Morning, and Two Pence for each Falk carried off."

The first Wesleyan chapel was built in the Old Jail Lane in 1816, to hold 800. And what do you think of this as a memorial to a Cobbold in St. Clement's Church? "To the memory of Thos. Cobbold, Common Brewer, who departed this life April 21, 1767, aged 59."

Christchurch Park was a beauty spot not to be missed and when Lord Rochester paid it a visit he noticed the park keeper was driving two donkeys attached to a large roller. The donkeys were wearing boots, so as not to damage the turf. This was thought to be a wonderful sight.

On the south wall of St. Mary Tower is a tablet to the famous Mrs. Cobbold of *Margaret Catchpole* fame. "As a public testimony of respect to exalted talents and unwearied exertions in the cause of benevolence and charity, this monument erected by the general concurrence of an extensive circle of friends, to the memory of Elizabeth Cobbold, the beloved wife of John Cobbold Esq. of Holy Wells. She died Oct. 17, 1824, aged 59." The comment runs: "Who can read these lines without feeling the truth of this elegant tribute to departed excellence; and who that has known the object of these praises can turn aside without dropping a tear of regret to her memory! Great indeed was her loss to the town of Ipswich."

One of the most interesting of Ipswich residents must have been W. H. Williams, M.D., who came to the town in 1801. In 1798 he invented Williams' field tourniquet, which was taken up by the Army Medical Board under the celebrated Duke of York, and issued to the troops: "to be employed in every regiment in the King's service, both at home and abroad, and the non-commissioned officers, drummers, and musicians, to be instructed in the use of it". Amongst his publications was one on the ventilation of army hospitals (shades of Florence Nightingale) and *Animadversions on certain Cases of Consumption and Dropsy treated by the Foxglove*.

Ipswich became the chief industrial town of Suffolk, with a special provision for an agricultural countryside. Because in the surrounding district was a vast corn-growing area, with attendant special needs. Ransome's iron foundry being the first.

Robert Ransome began activities in Norwich, but came here to seek his fortune in 1789 with the enormous capital of £200. It was at Ipswich in 1803 that he patented his cast-iron ploughshare that would remain sharp in use, and eventually ousted the steel share. He was joined in 1812 by Mr. William Cubitt, who was later to become one of the most famous engineers. Whilst in association they designed and built the old Stoke Bridge.

Then Charles May (both Ransome and May were Quakers) joined the partnership and they turned their attention to railway construction needs, soon to reach the town. In 1832 they produced the first lawn mower. (Previously lawns had been cut with a scythe.) In 1832 they excelled all others by producing the first self-moving steam engine, and in 1844 came the famous YL plough. In 1850–60 the firm, in co-operation with John Fowler, developed the latter's world-famous steam plough. Then, coming down the years, they produced the first-ever petrol-driven lawn mower.

At the first Royal Show that was held at Oxford in 1839, the only large exhibit was that of Ransomes who "sent up three waggons laden with more than six tons of machinery and implements, the superior manufacture and variety of which commanded universal approbation".

It must have been a friendly combination, and the name of Ransomes, Sims and Jefferies was to become known all over the world. In the very early days of the business it is said that on New Year's Eve, the workmen were supplied with bread, cheese and beer, employees and employers all joining in together. They would sit round the embers of the last furnace lighted in the old year, talking and laughing together.

Ransomes and Rapier were an offshoot of the first firm. They started in 1869 with two fitters, two porters and one labourer, and dealt in the lighter side of railway equipment. Just recently and having passed into other hands, they have removed to Sheffield, thus cutting a fine old Ipswich tradition of so many years.

The firm of E. R. and F. Turner commenced in 1837. Their first portable engine was exhibited at the Royal Agricultural Show at Norwich in 1849. It was a wonderful affair with a huge flywheel. They started at St. Peter's works in College Street, and amongst their possessions was the famous Wolsey Gate, the only visible memorial to the great cardinal left in his native town. This was presented to the town by them in 1929 and the cry went up: "What shall we do with it?"

Although Celia Fiennes commented that Ipswich failed to take advantage of its position on a river, all sorts of activities had been going on. Evidently she was in too much of a hurry to notice. There was malting, milling, brewing (not forgetting Thomas Cobbold, the *common* brewer) and shipbuilding. Later on Suffolk was in the van for scientific farming, and a firm like Packard, Chapman and Fison sprang up doing considerable export business in fertilizers. This was the outcome of the discovery of coprolites in East Suffolk. It is recorded that 1,000 tons of this fossilized excrement of carnivores were dug up out of a field behind the Maybush Inn at Waldringfield yearly.

James Fison, who farmed at Banningham, traded as a miller in

1780. His third son, who married Deborah Prentice, was also a miller at Stowmarket. It was his son Joseph who moved to Ipswich and founded the firm of Joseph Fison in 1847. Three nephews of Deborah founded the firm of Prentice Bros. in Stowmarket in 1856. An Edward Packard at this time in conjunction with Sir John Lawes of Rothampstead, was making researches into the manufacture of superphosphates. He established a business in 1849. These three business undertakings were united into one in 1929 as Fison, Packard and Prentice.

Linseed oil and oil cake for cattle were also made at Ipswich, and there were two large soap-boiling establishments. It was advisable to keep on the leeward side of these, although it reminds one of the despair felt by the lady. " 'A soap boiler,' cried the Duchess, feeling for her salts. 'I would sooner see every descendant of my house stretched in their graves than disgraced by a commercial alliance. It is the pride of my life that not one of my four daughters was allowed to marry lower than an earldom.' "

Then there were brickyards and kilns—making Suffolk pots of the best Suffolk earth—two clothing factories and a paper mill.

In 1869 there were four shipbuilding yards. They built many sightly two- and three-masted vessels. One of these, the *John Cobbold*, made voyages to China. In the seventies there were over fifty round-bottomed vessels hailing from the port, two- and three-masted schooners, brigs and barques. Sprit-sail barges were quite common.

Amongst the very old-established businesses is that of the Cliff Brewery, founded first at Harwich by Thomas Cobbold, who moved to Ipswich because the water supply of Harwich was unsatisfactory. Then in 1790 the business of W. A. and A. C. Churchman was founded. Their first venture was tobacco, but they soon saw that the future lay in cigarettes, which were introduced about 1857, not forgetting cigars. It should be remembered that in those days one bought the better kinds of cigarettes loose, by the ounce. They were also twice as thick and half as long again as their successors today; also they had a straw or cane mouthpiece.

Ipswich was also the centre for the manufacture of rickcloths, stacksheets, waterproof covers, sacks and bags, marquees and tents.

For many long years Ipswich race meetings held a prominent place in the 'Calendar'. Up to 1883 flat racing was held on the Nacton course, the meeting extending over two days. For the next twelve years a two-day fixture under National Hunt Rules was held, but it subsequently faded into a one-day fixture and finally petered out in 1911. The old course has now been built on.

Once upon a time all roads led to Bury St. Edmunds, to see and worship at the great shrine of the martyred king at the abbey. What a place it must have been, shining in the sun, amid the enamelled fields of West Suffolk. Here, too, was a river, a little stream that failed to reach the sea, so they gave it the heaven-ascending name of the Lark. There is a thirteenth-century bridge over it named the Abbot's Bridge, which carries part of the abbey wall with it, which latter was built by Henry the sacrist and completely enclosed the great abbey.

The Abbey Gate was the principal entrance and opened into the great court before the abbot's palace. The ruins within the enclosure are those of St. Edmund's, the third abbey church, consecrated about 1095.

St. Mary's Church, with its beautiful hammer-beam roof, contains the body of Mary Tudor, third daughter of Henry VII, widow of Louis XII of France and wife of Charles Brandon, Duke of Suffolk. Her remains were removed here at the dissolution of the monastery. However, since curiosity gets the better of reverence and respect, the tomb was opened in 1731 and some locks of her hair cut off.

The literary associations of Bury are strong and definite, beginning with Jocelin, the Boswell of the famous Abbot Samson, who was discovered by John Gage Rokewood before Carlyle made him into a popular character of a strong man. Rokewood had the original Latin text published by the Camden Society, and it was that edition that Carlyle used. Jocelin describes Samson as of middle stature, nearly bald, having a face neither round nor yet long, a prominent nose, thick lips, clear and heavy piercing eyes, ears of the nicest sense of hearing and arched eyebrows often shaved.

Next in order comes Lydgate, some two centuries later, who was also an inmate of the famous abbey. He was associated with

Caxton and became a disciple of Chaucer, to whom he submitted some of his manuscripts. Amongst his works are: *History, Siege and Destruction of Troy*, undertaken at the command of Henry IV but dedicated to his successor Henry V; *Fall of Thebes*, written as a continuation of the *Canterbury Tales*; *Life of St. Edmund*; and the *Fall of Princes*, wherein he declares himself

> Born in a village which is called Lidgate
> In olden time a famous castle town
> In Danes time it was beaten down
> Time when St. Edmund Martyr Maid and King
> Was slain at Hoxne.

John Harvey in *Gothic England* writes: "Though it is anachronistic to describe Lydgate as England's Poet Laureate, he undoubtedly held a like position, provided verse for official occasions over a long period and was certainly the chief Court poet from the death of Gower in 1408 until his own at a date in the early 1450s." And again: "... much as we may lament Lydgate's failure to supply even a passable imitation of Chaucer, it was to Lydgate nevertheless that English poetry looked for guidance."

Unlike Ipswich, Bury was subject to several great fires, and one in 1198 almost destroyed the shrine of "the glorious martyr Edmund". Here follows Jocelin's graphic description:

> There was a wooden platform between the shrine and the high altar, whereon stood two tapers, which the keepers of the shrine used to renew and stick together, by placing one candle upon the stump of another in a slovenly manner. Under this platform there were many things irreverently huddled together, such as flax and thread and wax, and various utensils. In fact, whatever was used by the keepers of the shrine was put there, for there was a door with iron gratings.
>
> Now, when these keepers of the shrine were fast asleep, on the night of St. Etheldreda, part of a candle that had been removed, and was still burning, fell, as we conjectured upon the aforesaid platform covered with rugs. Consequently, all that was near, above or below, began to burn rapidly, so much so that the iron gratings were at a white heat. And lo! the wrath of the Lord was kindled, but not without mercy, according to the saying, "In wrath remember mercy"; for just then the clock struck before the hour of matins, and the master of the vestry getting up, observed and noticed the fire. He

ran at once, and, striking the gong as if for a dead person, cried at the top of his voice that the shrine was consumed by fire.

We then, all running thither, found the fire raging wonderfully, and encircling the whole shrine, and almost reaching the woodwork of the church. Our young men, running for water, some to the well, some to the clock, some with their hoods, not without great labour, extinguished the force of the fire, and also stripped some of the altars upon the first alarm. And when cold water was poured upon the front of the shrine, the stones fell, and were reduced almost to powder. Moreover, the nails by which the plates of silver were affixed to the shrine started from the wood, which had been burnt underneath to the thickness of my finger, and the plates of silver were left dangling one from the other without nails. However, the golden image of the Majesty in front of the shrine, together with some of the stonework, remained firm and untouched, and brighter after the fire than it was before, for it was all of gold.

Some digging took place in the abbey grounds in 1903, when the chapter house was laid bare and in it six stone coffins of the abbots were discovered. These in order were those of Ording (abbot 1148–57), Sampson (1182–1212), Richard de Insula (1229–1234), Henry of Rushbrook (1235–48), Edmund de Walpole (1248–57), Hugo I (1157–80), next the door of the chapter house. Thus, with the single exception of Hugo II, who succeeded Sampson as abbot and was made Bishop of Ely in 1229, all the abbots who ruled over this great benedictine foundation for 100 years were buried in the chapter house built on this spot by Helyas the sacrist, Ording's nephew.

Numerous trades and callings had their streets and rows within the borough. The lavanders—washermen and fullers of cloth—dwelt near the South Gate, while the dyers used the running streams. Cooks' Row led into the great market place, where the linen drapers, mercers and spicers had rows of merchandise on the east, tanners and skinners and ironmongers on the west. There were besides within the market square rows occupied by cheese-mongers, butter merchants and poulterers, as well as stalls for butchers in the shambles and hog market. South of the square was Barbers' Row, leading into Cooks' Row. Whiting Street and Hatton Street still bear names which denote the quarters occupied by the whitening makers and hat manufacturers.

But one's mind goes to the Angel on Angel Hill, a lovely bit of an old ecclesiastical market town as ever could be found. It seems but natural that Dickens made it the scene of so much adventure for the immortal Pickwick. The place and the person form a perfect combination. Then, of course, Bury has memories of Corder and the Red Barn Mystery, with his death mask in Moyses Hall Museum, and his skin used as the binding of a book, *à la* Hitler. And, also unlike Ipswich, the streets are uniform, crossing at right angles, all because of a fire on 11th April 1608, Monday, when the Quarter Sessions were being held: ". . . and by negligence an oat-malthouse was set on fire; from whence in most strange and sudden manner, through fierce winds the fire came to the farthest side of the town, and as it went, left some streets and houses safe and untouched. The flame flew clean over many houses near it, and did great spoil to many fair buildings farthest off; and ceased not till it had consumed one hundred and sixty dwelling houses, besides others; and in damage of Wares and household-stuff to the full value of sixty thousand pounds." According to Kirby: "This accident . . . might possibly occasion . . . one agreeable circumstance, which is, the great regularity of the streets. For these are now seen cutting each other at right angles, which contribute much to the beauty of them, and as the town stands upon an easy accent, it deserves the enconium which an ancient writer has given of it, viz. 'That the sun shines not upon a town more agreeable in its situation.' "

The medieval market cross, erected in 1773 by Robert Adam, is now an art gallery, restored to the original Georgian design.

The town has had a long struggle to retain its individuality and its own particular character. There has been a ceaseless warfare between those who care and those who don't, the latter more concerned with big business. Expansion has been the great word, and in the early 1960s the Corporation of the County Councils suggested the town's then population of some 21,000 should be increased to 40,000. This has not yet been accomplished.★

From this it is quite evident that great dangers lie ahead, chiefly because the hitherto unspoilt east side of the town has been chosen for exploitation. The town centre is still Bury St. Edmunds at its

★ The population of Bury St. Edmunds in the 1981 census was recorded as 31,178; it is now (1987) about 36,000.

The Market Square, Bury St. Edmunds

best, reminiscent of its great past as the shrine of so young a king, who at 29 was "set among the high tides of the kalendar".

Turning to Framlingham, one's first thoughts rest on the castle, with its curtain walls, thirteen towers and brick chimneys. But I must confess that my steps lead me to the church and those magnificent tombs of the Howards and Mowbrays, some of which were removed here from Thetford at the Dissolution.

Have you ever wondered how they got here? Did they come in a great cavalcade at dead of night, torches burning; possibly under the light of a full moon? However it was, here they rest, including the body of Henry Howard, Earl of Surrey, the poet beheaded a day before Henry VIII died.

> My friend, the things that do attain
>   The happy life be these, I find:
> The riches left, not got with pain;
>   The fruitful ground, the quiet mind;
>
> The equal friend; no grudge, no strife;
>   No change of rule, nor governance;
> Without disease the healthy life;
>   The household of continuance.

It is almost incredible to realize how much a place like Framlingham is bound up with the history of England. The castle, built in the time of the Saxon Heptarchy, was the home of one of the great families who stood for chivalry. Its vast domains can be in part realized when the list is noted: Framlingham cum Saxted, Kelsale, Hacheston, Peasenhall, Bungay, Kettleburgh, Earl Soham, Cratfield, Hollesley cum Sutton, Staverton cum Bromeswell, Stonham, Walton cum Trimley, Dunningsworth, Hoo and the Hundred of Loes. Indeed the fields of Framlingham are deep in old forgotten wars, and it is nowhere surprising to find there a Red Rose Meadow, subject to an annual rent of those crimson petals.

But it is strange how facets of historical Framlingham come to life again centuries after they happened. In 1471 all those vast domains and wealth passed to a little girl of 4, Anne Mowbray, because her father was the last of his line. When she was 6 on

15th January 1477, she was married to Richard, second son of Edward IV, Duke of York. She died soon after, and her husband with his brother was smothered in the Tower, with the name of Tyrrel heading the list of the perpetrators. A few years back, on a building site in London's Barbican, a leaden cist was unearthed, containing the body of a little girl. It was decided this was none other than the little Anne Mowbray, who was soon re-interred in Westminster Abbey.

It is also interesting to note that after 1554 the castle was not considered good enough as a permanent residence for nobility, the standard of living having that much improved. A century later it passed out of the hands of the noble family who had held it so long, by money, something never dreamed of when Sir Robert Hitcham bought it for £14,000. He in turn passed it to the masters, fellows and scholars of Pembroke College, Cambridge. He lies with the noble dust in the chancel.

Once upon a time there was a rhyme current which ran:

> Here lies Sir Robert Hitcham,
>   Old John Hitcham's son,
> Who about the town of Framlingham
> Carried many a bunch of broom.

Suffolk families were well connected. For example, Surrey's widow married secondly, Francis Steyning of Woodbridge, by whom she had a daughter, Mary, the wife of Charles Seckford, M.P. for Aldeburgh, 1572.

Sir Hitcham's thoughts were for ever turned towards the poor, hence his almshouses in Framlingham as also in Levington, his birthplace. But he was not alone in this interest, because Thomas Mills also distributed his money in this way, building more almshouses. An early historian suggested this did the township no good, because, what with other charities, it caused an influx of paupers to see what they could get.

Thomas Mills had the novel idea of being buried in his own garden, without any office or form, because he was a Dissenter.

When the plague came to Framlingham in 1666, the Market Hill was completely covered with grass.

Sudbury on the Stour, once noted for velvets and fine hangings, was another of Suffolk's delightful little towns. Here, as all the world knows, was the birthplace of Gainsborough. His statue by Bertram Mackennal faces the Market Hill of his earliest home.

Gainsborough's romantic looking house, with its rounded wing and conical roof has been restored and has become a study centre not only for the artist's work but of the eighteenth-century culture of his times. The Gainsborough House Society holds exhibitions there and has built up a library of works relating to the painter.

A portrait of the Gravenor family of Ipswich, painted by Gainsborough about 1748 when he was 21, made the astonishing price of £280,000 at Sotheby's in 1972. This was a world auction record for any English work of art. The previous record for a Gainsborough was £130,000 paid in 1960 for the portrait of Mr. and Mrs. Robert Andrewes which is in the National Gallery. The picture, about three feet square, was sent to the sale room by two members of the Townsend family to whom it had passed. They always looked upon it as a fake.

The best of Sudbury's ancient houses is Salter's Hall in Stour Street.

Standing as it does on a river, Sudbury possesses a stone bridge of some significance. The original bridge, or what is supposed to have been the original, was swept away by a flood on 4th November 1520, but it was rebuilt the next year. Dr. Taylor, the Hadleigh Martyr, passed over it in 1555 in the custody of the sheriff.

But Sudbury's chief claim to fame in these modern times, lay in the removal of Ballingdon Hall, built in the sixteenth century, 1,000 yards on an S-bend route—and uphill at that—to a new site, because the original position was spoilt by reason of a new development. This fine old mansion was originally built on an H-plan, by a member of the Paston family, who early in its life conveyed it to Thomas Eden, Clerk to the Star Chamber, in whose family it remained for many generations.

Curiously enough, within recent years, it was put up for auction, and the gipsies bought it. When S. R. Jones was gathering material for his excellent book *England East*, this is what he found:

"The sides of an unkempt drive were strewn with gypsies, dozens of them, women, youths, girls, babies innumerable, mostly sprawled outside caravans and tents around fires boiling sizzling pots. The hall showed at the end of the drive." When he asked permission to go inside, he was politely told he could go where he liked, and stay as long as he wished. It is now about a sixth of its previous size, because in earlier years it was the chief baronial house in the neighbourhood.

Leiston is a small town with a very large outlook. Eastward is that formidable-looking pile known as Suffolk's first atomic power station. But in the very heart of the small place is Leiston Works.

The name of Garrett must be for ever associated with Leiston. The first Richard Garrett was a blacksmith who emigrated from Woodbridge and opened a small engineering works here in 1778. He was one of the first in England to specialize in agricultural machinery. His son, another Richard, married a daughter of a man named John Balls, also a blacksmith, who is believed to have designed the first threshing machine. So the strain of invention and creation must have run strongly in the descendants.

Their chief contribution was the development of the threshing machines. They also made an expensive range of other agricultural machinery such as that for haymaking, horse hoes, manure barrels, stone mills, cake crushers, chaff cutters, rollers, ploughs, barley hummellers, winnowers and dressers. They also made those iron mushroom-shaped rick stands, known as stringalls after J. Stringall of Ipswich, who invented them. They were also known as 'striddles' or 'stathels'.

However, not the least important feature of their manufactures was the steam boiler, a branch in which they became justly famous. The boiler shops, with their immense plate-heating furnaces, punching, rolling, and hydraulic flanging machines, and powerful steam riveting machines "must be seen to appreciate the magnitude of their utility".

Some years ago I was shown a log-book of an old carpenter at Westleton, a member of a very old and respected family of the village, bearing an honoured name. In it I had a rather interesting find, in an invitation circular, partly printed and partly written with the flourish of those years. It was dated Leiston, 12th January 1841 and read:

Sir,

Friday the 22nd inst, being the day fixed for my Annual Meeting, to be held at the White Horse Inn, Leiston, I hope to have the pleasure of your Company.

Dinner will be ready at 2 o'clock, but I respectfully solicit your early attendance that we may arrange our business previous to the dinner hour.

Mr Rous,   I remain, Sir,
        Carpenter,   Yours most respectfully,
                Westleton.   Rc. Garrett.

It is not difficult to picture the scene at the White Horse, and to hear the Suffolk intonation as they met to eat, and incidentally whet their whistles. Or even smell the smell of the dinner in preparation. One feels that Mr. Rous must have enjoyed it all and looked forward to the next. But as paper was scarce in those days, the invitation provided Mr. Rous with two clean pages that he was quick to use in the drafting of a bill for work done for a Mr. Teacon. Amongst the items was one of interest: "July 24. To repairing Lukum window at Browns. Stuff nails and work 2/-." No signs of inflation in those days but the 'lukum' was none other than Suffolk parlance for a dormer. The "Bill made" was £7 13s. 7½d., and there was an allowance of 3s. for beer.

Some twenty-odd years ago an old Leistonian revisited the little town and recorded his reminiscences.

When I left Leiston the Station Works was a mass of timber stacks and the White Horse meadow stocked full of engines and thrashing tackle. When I realized there was no 'bull' to wake me at 6 o'clock the morning. Anyhow it was Saturday morning. I lay in bed and recalled those Saturday mornings of nearly half a century ago when at 12 o'clock hundreds of men were paid at the gates as they left the works. At least the charge-hands paid in little tins which they used to throw back into the baskets of the tally boys, young beginners who used to hand us checks through the peep-holes as we went to work. We used to stand about in groups, completely blocking Main Street, while the charge hands doled out the Gang's money. What Saturday mornings they were, and what bartering went on around the ornamental gardens and the Post Office Square. I wonder what some men would think to-day of working from 6 a.m. to 8 p.m. and all Friday night, and then think themselves lucky if they earned a quid.

When I was young and we had to look at every penny, it was possible to get a ticket to Aldeburgh, on the old Great Eastern Railway for 8s. for eight days.* There was never such an occasion passed without noticing the various bits of agricultural machinery packed up in Russian mats, standing on the loading quay at the station, labelled for Russia and South America. Incidentally, those old mats were used when removing household furniture and smelt delightfully.

Again, there were those little traction engines, made by the firm, running smoothly and shiningly along the roads, labelled Richard Garrett and Sons, Leiston. They were used for hauling guns in the First World War, but now have become period pieces all.

The firm's activities could also be seen in all kinds of bits and pieces of iron work about the countryside. Such as girders for little bridges over streams; even iron grave memorials instead of headstones. These latter can be found in Westleton and Wrentham churchyards.

Stowmarket, another manufacturing town, even to that of making gunpowder, has memories of John Milton, who is alleged to have planted the mulberry tree which straddled in the garden of the former vicarage, a shoot of which still bears. He came here to be tutored by Thomas Young, whose memorial in the fourteenth-century church is said to have been composed by his pupil.

> Here is committeed to earth's trust
> Wise, pious, spotless, learned dust,
> Who, living, more adorned the place,
> Than the place him; such was God's grace.

Originally the Saxon Thorney, the town became the one market of the Hundred of Stow, therefore Stowmarket. Here were held the mote, and for many years meetings for the nomina-

* Allan Jobson was writing of the 1890s. Aldeburgh lost the trains in 1959.

tion, and sometimes the election, of Members of Parliament for the county.

Prosaic as Stowmarket may be today—although it has an ambitious rural life museum—yet like Woolpit it was once a place where fairies danced in the streets, notably in Tavern Street, a name which may appear significant for such happenings. No less a person than Holinshed vouches for them, though a local man was going home one bright moonlight night when he saw them. In his own words:

> There might be a dozen of them, the biggest about three feet high, the small ones like dolls. Their dresses sparkled as if with spangles like the girls at shows at Stow Fair; they came moving round hand in hand in a ring; no noise [came] from them. They seemed light and shadowy, not like solid bodies. I passed on, saying "The Lord have mercy on me" but them must be the fairies, and being alone there on the path over the field could see them as plain as I do you. I looked after them when I got over the stile, and they were there just the same, moving round and round. . . . I might be forty yards from them, and I did not like to stop and stare at them. I was quite sober at the time.

In 1586 Mr. John Hare, by will, left a sum of money derived from a tenement in Crow Street, for the sexton: ". . . at the time accustomed to ring the greatest bell in the steeple, at Stowmarket, and in the morning also to raise up and awaken the artificers there dwelling".

Amongst the records of old crafts, it is interesting to recall that the earliest known basket-maker in England was Johannes Hoo of Stowmarket. He was assessed 3s. in the Suffolk Poll Tax, dated 1381: "Johanne Hoo basket maker *cum* Margeria *uxore et* Cecelia *matre.*" Hoo is an ancient name, and the family is said to have settled in this country before the Norman Conquest.

Needham Market (Anglo-Saxon, 'a home in need') passed into a proverb: "You are in the highway to Needham," which Fuller elaborates:

> Needham is a market town in this county, well stocked(if I mistake not) with poor people; though I believe this in no way did occasion

the first denomination thereof. They are said to be in the highway to Needham who hasten to poverty.

However, these fall under a distinction; some go, others are sent thither. Such as go embrace several ways; some, if poor, of idleness: if rich, of carelessness, or else of Prodigality.

Others sent thither against their wills by the powerful oppression of such who either detain or devour their estates. And it is possible some may be sent thither by no fault of their own, or visible cause from others, but merely from divine justice, insensibly dwindling their estate chiefly for trial of their patience.

Wherefore, so many ways leading to Needham from divers quarters, I mean from different causes; it is unjust to condemn all persons meeting there, under the censure of the same guiltiness.

But folks of our modern generation go to see the church roof, one of the finest in Suffolk. Ingeniously constructed to bridge a wide span, it dates from the latter half of the fifteenth century and is quite unique. It is unique also in that the clerestory is made of wood. Up to Victorian times it was all cased in by a domed plaster ceiling.

A building in the little town was used by the strolling players, and E. W. Platten in his little book, tells of Johnny Hayward, who said: "I once climbed the ruff, master, and see the Mask fur nawthen'." The old post office in 1840 consisted of three cottages, one bore the sign: "Small beer sold here penny a pint."

The congregational minister in 1755 was a young student, the Reverend John Priestley, who was in receipt of £30 per annum. He was a Greek scholar and scientist, being the discoverer of oxygen gas.

Once upon a time was exhibited this notice: "Whereas several idle fellows have robbed the river at Pipps. The game and fish laws will be rigorously enforced against all those that shall in any way offend, 1776."

The principal trade was wool combing, not weaving. This was lost when the plague came to the town and never regained. The sick and poor pest house at the bottom of Bridge Street is a reminder of this. Wool combing, by the way, was done with large combs that were heated in a charcoal fire. The fleeces were stretched across on wires or ropes.

Hadleigh (Anglo-Saxon *heltega*, 'health meadow') is an old

town, boasting an old foundation. Etymologically, it derives from head-piece, and was of considerable importance even in Saxon times. Guthrum the Danish leader, captured by Alfred and graciously pardoned on condition that he became a Christian, made this his headquarters, died and was buried here, thus creating it a royal town. It was early given over to the manufacture of cloth, which was established by the reign of Edward I, as indeed were its neighbours of Lavenham and Sudbury. Holinshed records a rebellion that broke out here in 1526, owing to the conditions in the weaving industry. The festival of Bishop Blaize was celebrated up to the early years of the nineteenth century.

Situated on the south side of the churchyard, the guildhall forms a picturesque feature of a most unusual collection of buildings with the church and the deanery tower within the precincts of a parish churchyard. Here, in more senses than one, is the historic part of this old woollen centre expressed in three contemporary but distinct types of buildings, timber framing for the guildhall, brick for the tower, flint and ashlar for the church.

The deanery tower a smaller copy of that erected by Edmund Beddingfield at Oxburgh in Norfolk, was built by William Pykenham in 1495. Of old red brick it is 43 feet 5 inches high to the top of the battlements and 31 feet 4 inches wide. Underneath was a passageway to the old rectory. Pykenham intended to build a rectory to correspond, but was prevented by death.*

It was in the oratory of this tower that saw the birth of the Tracts for the Times, which ushered in the Oxford Movement. Hugh James Rose was then in his short ministry and here came his friends, William Palmer, Froude and Arthur Percivall, to discuss the best means to be adopted to stir up the dying embers of the English Church. Rose also built the present deanery.

Of the church itself, the tower is earlier than the remainder and rises to 64 feet in height, while the spire, covered with sheets of lead, is another 71 feet. Most of these tall spires, erected in the thirteenth century, have since fallen, but this is an interesting survival. Another interesting item is the external clock bell, the

---

* An overmantel painted by the young Thomas Gainsborough in 1748–50 shows a large timber-framed house as the rectory behind Archdeacon Pykenham's gate tower. The painting is on loan to Gainsborough's House, Sudbury.

oldest amongst the bells since it is known to have been in its present position since 1584. It is inscribed in Lombardic characters: "*Ave Maria Gracia Plena Dominis Tecum*", the letters, by a mistake in casting, being the wrong way round.

Hadleigh ringers possessed one of those gotches, of which there were several in the county. It was round, $15\frac{1}{2}$ inches high, $14\frac{1}{2}$ across the handles, had two ears and held 16 quarts. It was inscribed: "ME. Thomas Windle, Isaac Bvnn, John Mann, Adam Sage, George Bond, Thomas Goldsborough, Robart Smith, Henry West." Then follows:

> If you love me due not lend me,
> Eves me often and keep me clenly,
> Fill me full or not at all
> If it be strong, and not with small.

Happily, after wandering in private ownership, the jug has been returned to the church, its real home.

That Hadleigh ringers possessed such a pot is hardly to be wondered, since it was a rector of Hadleigh, John Still, D.D. who is credited with the drinking song:

> I cannot eat but little meat
>   My stomach is not good;
> But sure I think that I can drink
>   With him that wears a hood.
> Though I go bare, take ye no care,
>   I am nothing a cold;
> I stuff my skin so full within,
>   Of jolly good ale and old.
> Back and sides go bare, go bare,
>   Both foot and hand go cold:
> But, belly, God send thee good ale enough,
>   Whether it be new or old.

Perhaps the most interesting thing in the church is in the south chapel of St. John the Evangelist, in a wooden bench-end. This represents a beast sitting down on its hindquarters, holding in its mouth the head of a man by its hair. The beast's head is covered with a hood, kept in position by a liripipe, or small pendant tail of the hood, tied as a fillet round the brow. The neck is enriched with a collar, resembling the ornaments worn by ecclesiastics on their robes; and on its back is a vestment. Its forefeet are encased in shoes of Richard II period, while the hind feet are cloven. This represents the finding of St. Edmund's head by a wolf according to the legend, and is thought to be a masterly caricature of the monks of the abbey at Bury.

Hadleigh is chiefly famous for its sons, either by birth or adoption, the latter to be found in its more distinguished rectors. These include Rowland Taylor, whom Fuller described as having the merriest and pleasantest wit. Then there was John Still, the reputed author of *Gammer Girtin's Needle.* The Reverend William Hawkins, master of the free grammar school, housed at that time, it is thought, in the old guildhall. He composed *Apollo Shriving*, performed by the boys on Shrove Tuesday, 7th February 1626. A passage in this is supposed to have provided John Milton with an idea regarding Eve in *Paradise Lost*:

> The clouds do from her presence flye
> 'Tis sunshine where she casts her eye;
> Where're she treads on earth below
> A rose or lily up doth grow.
> Her breath a gale of spieces brings;
> Mute are her Muses, when she sings.

Then came Dr. Cottesford, who from the cure of souls turned to the cure of bodies. "Dr. Cottesford suffered much for the Royal cause, and being never able to obtain his fifths from his successor [that is the portion of tithe which he was allowed by law to a deprived incumbent], was constrained to take upon him the practise of Physick at Ipswich, where he died a few years after, very poor."

Dr. Trumball was another. He administered the last rites to Archbishop Sancroft at Fressingfield. "The Archbishop took especial care that a juror should not perform the burial service over him, and even appointed by name the person whom he desired to officiate. The day before he died [23rd November 1693] he received the Sacraments from Dr. Trumball, who had formerly been his chaplain and who was a non-juror."

Two others who were educated at the grammar school: John

Overall, born at Hadleigh in 1560, and John Baise, both Cambridge scholars, took a prominent part in the translation of the Bible into the Authorized Version of 1611. Overall compiled the questions and answers on the Sacraments at the end of the Church Catechism. William Alabaster (1567–1640), born at Hadleigh of an old merchant family, was educated at Westminster School and Trinity College, Cambridge, where his Latin play, *Roxane*, was written and first acted. And lastly, Thos. Woolner, sculptor and poet, was born here in 1825.

Hadleigh has also a fine bridge, Topesfield Bridge, that spans the Stour; as also the mill, which dates its foundation from Domesday when "A free woman Lavena held two caracutes as a manor, five acre meadow, and one mill".

Hadleigh was at one time the centre for crêpe-making, and hops were cultivated in its fields. For as Bullein remarks in his *Government of Health*: "... tho' goodly stilles and fruitful grounds of England do bring forth unto man's use, as good hops as groweth in any place in this world, as by proof I know in many places in the countie of Suffolke, whereas they brew their own beere with the hops that grow upon their own ground."

Southwold was the scene of the boys' camp inaugurated by the Duke of York, who later became King George VI. The boys were his guests for a week of the then August Bank Holiday. They were drawn from public and elementary schools from all over the country. The great feature was the visit of the Duke, who shared in all the life, the only difference being he was allowed an iron bedstead in his tent. It was a great institution and lasted for eight summers.

The Villages

As one who long in populous city pent,
Where houses thick and sewers annoy the air,
Forth issuing on a summer's morn to breathe
Among the pleasant villages and farms
Adjoin'd, from each thing met conceives delight.

Milton

Suffolk is so rich in its villages, some 500 of them. In many respects they hold time in suspense, although it has been suggested that some of the smaller villages are in danger of dying. Having lasted so many generations with their Anglo-Saxon names, it is to be hoped they will last until planners cease to plan. Failing that, we must use again the last words of Marie Antoinette: "A moment more, executioner, a moment more."

Most of the buildings date from Tudor and Elizabethan times, with their age-old baulks, brick and plaster filling, called into being by the Dissolution of the Monasteries and the general re-distribution of land. They reflect centuries of varying fortunes and a sturdy independent, self-contained village life, centred on the church, about the walls of which the fathers sleep. Crafts-manship is everywhere, in a bit of carving here, a chimney stack there, window frame, doorway or overhang. And a bit of work for the church in chest or screen, in which the arts combine to blossom as the rose. You can find it everywhere, in out-of-the-way corners, at a bend in the road and the least expected of places. Indeed, wherever man has called a home into existence from the materials that were immediately to hand, such as clay-lump on the heavy lands.

Take for example Cratfield, an out-of-the-way village on a tributary of the Waveney, with a population of 673 in 1855 which had shrunk to 564 by 1871. Yet this small community could

The Water Pump, Westleton village green

produce one of the most beautiful of the Seven Sacrament Fonts in the kingdom, a work of supreme art dating from the latter half of the fifteenth century. Its design and execution must be seen to be believed, with always the possibility that originally it was coloured.

How did it all come about, so lovely an adornment in a village church? Who made it? Did it come there waterborne on the wavelets of the little tributary, possibly then a broader stream? What a sight it must have been in all its pristine glory, the gift of a great soul for the beginning of life of Cratfield boys and girls. How it must have shone in the sunlight that came in through those old windows.

Accidents occurred and man's elemental fear of fire was for ever in a villager's mind. Suckling in his history has this: "On Sunday, April 18, 1736, Carlton Hall bake-house, barn and stables were burnt down by a foul chimney taking fire." This reminds me of the old Suffolk riddle:

> Black within,
> Red without,
> Four corners,
> Like a clout.   (A chimney.)

Neither should it be forgotten that it was at a Suffolk village, Wetheringsett, that Hakluyt's *Voyages* was produced. It appears there were two Richard Hakluyts, cousins, who collaborated in this, but it was the Suffolk Richard who provided the maps of an Elizabethan fairyland, complete with savages, wigwams, flying dolphins, wide rivers, ships in sail, tall trees, and all the wonders of the seven seas unknown to anyone who was not a sailor. Surely some of the wonderful figures on the bench-ends of Suffolk churches are due to this romanticized outlook on the unknown.

Here is the record to be found in an old manorial account of Icklingham, 1342–3:

Cost of the houses and walls. In 1 carpenter being hired making a new chamber at the end of the hall 18d. Also in 1 cooper being hired for coopering the same and daubing the walls 18d. [Cooper: a name evidently used in an Anglo-Saxon sense, and here meaning a thatcher.] In bolts and hinges bought for the door of the same chamber 2d. Also one lock and key bought for the same door 1½d. In a key bought for the door, 2d. In 1 manger made for the horses eating therefrom in the same chamber, 3d. In boards bought for the same, namely of oak, 5d. In 1 cooper being hired for three days coopering and putting a ridge on the grange, 7½d. (taking daily 2½d). In 1 garcon being hired waiting upon the same time, 3½d. In twigs bought for binding the thatch upon the house and making springles thereof 2d. In coopering and putting ridges on the walls in divers places, for three days and a half, 7d.

These villages are a veritable harvest, the flowering of a fine English tradition of hand labour, expressing honest purpose. These modest homes, often neglected in past years, have suddenly come into their own, and cost as much today as a whole mansion with woodland acres of a few years ago. What a delightful vignette they make, with their sportive gardens, or an espalier pear or plum clinging to the colour-washed walls.

Of course there were great houses in these villages, as Queen Elizabeth I very well knew. She was glad to make a splendid progress along our flower-bordered, gritty and rutted roads to, say, Long Melford or Hengrave. I wonder if there were any springs to her state carriages? It is interesting to note how Thomas Kitson seems to have dealt in "wool, Venese gynger, sugar, copper, cornish tyn, cloth, velvet, hoppys, canvas, soape". Indeed much of English history centres about the villages of England and Suffolk in particular. Mary Tudor attended Westhorpe Church, and the chapel at the end of the south aisle was known as Mary Tudor's pew.

Goods and chattels were cherished, handed on and down—not least the stock in the yard and the wagons that lumbered through the miry roads. This extract from the will of Robert Leget of Icklingham St. James, 1534, is suggestive of much: "Item to the said John Leget iij horses one black called Colle an other called amblinge horse & a dune horse the thiller with the harnes longinge to them. Itm. to John my sonne my best vyolet cote and my wusted dublet. Item a cart bodye with a payre of newe wheeles unshod I will that John my sonne shall shoe one whele & my wife Maryan the other whele afore harvest come. Itm. I will that John my sonne shall helpe my wife Maryan in with her harvest & to see that she have right for knowledge of her lands."

Thomas Neve, 1532, gave to "Thomas his eldest sonne his best kettle, and to his son William his best brasse pott & one kettle & his greene coat".

Margerie Berre, 1526, bequeathed "to Marian Morledge a hanginge posuet a Kettell with a bell candlestick a flock bedde my beste kercheffe save one a vyolett kirtle".

John Allen, 1511, bequeathed to "Constance my wyff and to her assignes all such stuff goodes and hostalament of houshold that was hers before my marriage that be not spent nor worne in owe time and also she have a sylur peace with a covering and a little sylur salt which was hirs before my tyme".

Alicia Dyx, 1503: "I gyve & bequeatehe my tabyl mad of ij plankes & my grett cheyr to remayne wt the sayd place as longe as they endure." Also "my led & qwerne standying in the bakehouse & my grett fatt & my huche".

John Thompson, Rector of Icklingham, made his will: "In the year of our lord god 1556, and in the third and fourth yeres of the Reygne of our Lord an Lady Phylyp and Mary by the grace of god Kyng and Queene of Ingland, Spayne, France both scycylles Jerusalem and Ireland."

Richard Bryghtholde, 1557: "I bequethe to the chylde wherewith my wfe now goeth if it be borne into the world and live to Michaelmas next after the date threof xxxiijs iiijd to be payde to my wfe at the said feast." He also left "one bedde with all thereto belongynge that is to say a Transom ij pyllowes a coverlet a payre of shetes ij testuris with hangngs and all this at hir owne choyce one bigger than other & one latten candlestycke iij pewter plattes besyde that which she brought in with hyr, one great coffer in the chamber nexte the strete & one brasse pott the best that she will chose with all hyr lynen apparell & other thyngs which she brought with her".

But George Stanton of Icklingham, clerk, 21st March 1655, left "Ten little volumes conteyning the hebrew byble and Greeke testament be reserved for my sonne Thomas".

At the village of Acton once stood Acton Place, seat of the Daniels family. This was sold to Robert Jennens, *aide* to the Duke of Marlborough, by his son William, who became the richest man of his time, but something of a miser. He died intestate at the age of 97. He had been a page to George I. At his death Acton

Place was dismantled, the tapestry torn from the walls and sold. There was a room called the Point Room from being hung with point needlework; another was the Silk Room. Amongst the curiosities was a bed, presented by William III, which, it is said, was lined with royal shirts.

When Melford Hall was the home of Lord Savage, James Howell was there as a tutor and wrote this delightful letter to a friend—an account of a Suffolk nobleman's home:

My dear Dan-Though considering my former condition of life I may now be called a countryman, yet you cannot call me a rustic, as long as I live in so civil and noble a family, as long as I lodge in so virtuous and regular a house as any I believe in the land, both for aeconomical government and the choice company; for I never saw such a dainty race of children in all my life together: I never saw yet such an orderly and punctual attendance of servants, nor a great house so neatly kept: here one shall see no dog nor cat nor cage to cause any nastiness within the body of the house. The kitchen and gutters and other offices of noise and drudgery are at the fag end; there's a back gate for the beggars and the meaner sort of swains to come in at. The stables butt on the park, which for chearful rising ground, for groves and browsing ground for the deer, for runlets of water, may compare with any for its highness in the whole land. It is opposite to the front of a great house, whence from the gallery one may see much of the game when they are hunting. Now for the gardening and choice of flowers, for fruits of all sorts, there are few the like in England. Here you have your Bon Christian pears and Bergamot in perfection; your Muscatel grapes in such plenty that there are some bottles of wine sent every year to the king; and one to Mr. Daniel, a worthy gentleman hard by, who hath been long abroad, makes a good store of his vintage. Truly this house of Long Melford, tho' it be not so great, yet it is so well compacted and contrived with such dainty conveniencies every way, that if you saw the landskip of it you would be mightily taken with it, and it would serve for a choice pattern to build and contrive a house by.

May 20, 1619.   Yours J.H.

In the summer of 1842 Jane Carlyle visited Mrs. Bullen at Troston. (She was the mother of Thomas Carlyle's former pupil.) She remarked it was a quiet life there, conducted with such ethical propriety that on Sunday when out for a drive in the evening

Mr. Bullen always *walked* the horse on principle, and Jane could not evade the church service officiated by Reginald whose manner of delivery left room for improvement. She represented him as pausing just when he needed a breath, at the end of a sentence or in the middle of a word as it happened.

Some of the cottage homes as I knew them were extremely beautiful by any standards, full of nice little bits of furniture of which they thought nothing. How they laughed when people came in and went mad with jealousy over a planked-top table. "Yis, thass some old, whoi we used tew have thet in our barn for the bags of corn to rest on." To say nothing of the bits and pieces of lustre ware, such as a jug a sailor son had brought home from Sunderland:

The Sailors Tear

He leap'd into the boat
As it lay upon the strand;
But, oh! his heart was far away,
With friends upon the land
He thought of those he lov'd the best
A wife and infant dear,
And feelings fill'd the sailor's breast
The sailor's eye a tear.

Or it might be a 'pudden plate' of salt glaze, with tear-drop edge. How they came by these things seems almost curious, but they were not exactly treasured, and yet they survived. In some more sophisticated households they were kept out of sight of prying eyes.

No room downstairs would have been complete without a grandfather clock, bearing the name of a local maker. These latter seem to have been legion, because a list was attempted some years ago but never completed. What a pleasant sonorous tick they had, as leisurely as the days which brought them to birth. Oh! and there might have been a silhouette, or a wood engraving of the local church in an Oxford frame.

Neither must one forget the village pub. Kirton on the Deben possessed two, the 'White Horse' and the 'Greyhound'. Now alas, and only yesterday, the older of the two, the 'Greyhound', also known colloquially as 'The Dog', has entirely vanished. They used to keep the band instruments there, and the practice night that beat all records was on the first Friday in February, a free night, as being the nearest to the landlord's birthday. There was a poacher's gun hung up in the parlour. It had a ball underneath the trigger that could be pumped up, this giving eighteen silent shots for one inflation.

Redgrave, which was a mother parish to Botesdale on the borders between East and West Suffolk, and was on one of the old coach routes, had no less than four inns. The 'Greyhound', kept by a blacksmith in 1879, the 'Cross Keys', the 'Fox and Hounds' and the 'Bunch of Grapes'.

There were also all kinds of curios amongst the parsons, such as at the village of Falkenham. He was a wild fowler, and if a flock of geese came up the river during church time, he was off—"sarvice or no sarvice". He administered discipline but did not receive it.

Stradbroke, with its church gleaming like a jewel amid the surrounding fields, had a son, the learned Robert Grosseteste, Bishop of Lincoln. In the churchyard rests another of its inhabitants, rather below the standard of the future bishop. He was James Chambers, a queer itinerant, ragged follower of the Muse, who, scorning comfort, preferred its opposite and wrote:

> This vile raiment hangs in tatters;
> No warm garment to defend:
> O'er my flesh the chill snow scatters;
> No snug hut!—no social friend!

He lies under an inscription to "The poor patient, wandering Suffolk poet."

This is what Munro Cautley had to say about Cookley: "This church is chiefly remarkable as the scene of a shocking restoration so late as 1894. The rood screen was demolished and carted to the rectory stables at Huntingfield and most probably burnt, the box-pews were distributed in the village to mend hen houses."

At Fressingfield, in the manor of Willingham Hall, lived 'Fair Margaret', who was so beautiful that she beguiled the heart of Prince Edward, later to become Edward I. It is said the prince, hunting from his forest at Framlingham, tired and thirsty, found himself at Fressingfield, to discover he had run down a quarry fairer than he could dream. Upon being recalled by his father, he left her in charge of the Earl of Lincoln, who in turn married her himself. Such were her charms, however, that it is said two other knights fought to the death for her favours, one being of Cratfield, the other of Laxfield.

Gone are the days of the lord of the manor, freeholders alias yeomanry, copyholders, cottagers, squatters, farm servants. Yet the village still lives on, a very different community to that of even pre-Second World War. Some have become dormitories of the towns, or a refuge from the stress and strain of modern life, because here is to be found:

> An English home, grey twilight poured
>   On dewy pastures, dewy trees,
> Softer than sleep,—all things in order stored,
>   A haunt of ancient Peace.

During the short period since this book was first issued, many of the happenings forecast in the last chapter have taken place. Felixstowe has become the second largest container port in the country, and the Southern Relief Road has come into being. All the bypasses have been made.

Turning to other matters, the old Tide Mill at Woodbridge has been restored and turned into a gallery for the Arts. The old Corn Exchange at Ipswich has also been restored and was re-opened as an Entertainments and Arts Centre by their Royal Highnesses the Duke and Duchess of Gloucester. Then, sad to relate, we have lost a number of our very eminent citizens, including Benjamin Britten, who was not only a citizen but a son. There has also been a laudable movement to bring back the Village School.

Suffolk's Tomorrow

Boast not thyself of tomorrow; for thou knowest not what a day may bring forth.

Proverbs

In a mutable atmosphere no one can tell what is next. When changes are sprung upon us with the morning milk and such age-old institutions as County Sessions, civic and local governments are outmoded, one may well ask, "What next?" That Suffolk has a future is very certain and it is good to realize that its boundaries, with the exception of five parishes near Great Yarmouth, are to be those settled by our Saxon forefathers, rather than an outline drawn in some distant office. Once upon a time, in the romantic days of yesterday, they used to say that East Anglia's capital city, Dunwich, now under the grey waters, had golden gates. Now it is the county of Suffolk as a whole that takes upon itself the title of the 'Golden Gateway' for Europe.

Just as a revolution in living has come to our villages in the form of sanitation, piped water, electricity, telephones and television, and in so doing has swept away age-old traditions, the old secluded self-contained existence has gone also. So new things, new ways, new machines crop up to make life that much more complicated and difficult. Apart from the decision to enter the Common Market, the outstanding development of the area has been the discovery of natural gas beneath the North Sea.

The year 1974 brought an important change for Suffolk, in the form of a single county council. This amalgamation or union was proposed as long ago as 1889 by Lord Gwydyr of Stoke Park, Ipswich, when the Local Government Act was introduced. In moving a resolution proclaiming that the union of the two councils was desirable for the greater efficiency and economy to county management, he deplored the fact that the then very

The Quay Theatre

influential Marquess of Bristol should have managed to persuade the House of Lords, in face of opposition from other Suffolk peers, to amend the Bill then under discussion, which had proposed one county. He went on to say: "Thus the wants and wishes of the vast majority of the inhabitants and ratepayers of Suffolk were completely sacrificed to a small minority living in and around Bury." He was a firm believer that a county prospered best while remaining undivided in its interests and aims.

Incidentally Lord Gwydyr was a remarkable man who lived to a great age. He was born in 1810, and as a boy of 10 he went in his grandfather's state barge to Westminster and watched from a gallery George IV's coronation. He was also a spectator of the crowning of William IV and took part in the coronation of Queen Victoria when he was official secretary to the Lord Great Chamberlain, a post he held until 1870.

What this dual local government has meant to Suffolk can now be seen in the constitution of the new council, which will consist of eighty-one councillors, eighteen of them from Ipswich. This represents a sweeping reduction, because East Suffolk previously had ninety-three, West Suffolk seventy, and Ipswich fifty-six. It should be noted, however, that Ipswich governed its own affairs because the borough council has had the same powers as the county council, plus those of smaller towns and districts.

There are of course dangers looming ahead in this very large organization, because some can see a loss of human relationships. This new county council is the largest employer of labour, as teachers, technicians, roadmen, social workers, planners, lawyers, architects and others will number some 20,000. Moreover the council is responsible for spending some 50 millions of the ratepayers' money.

Making Suffolk a better place in which to live is the aim and object of the Suffolk Rural Community Council, a most excellent institution, skilfully run. This covers a wide field of exploration and experiment in carrying out its work, which started in 1937. For example the R.C.C. has provided the secretariat for the two Suffolk Parish Councils' Associations.

This has meant that the parish council has changed from a virtually moribund body to one which is aware of its powers and duties and has no hesitation in making its voice heard whenever it feels the interests of the parish are concerned. Its value has been acknowledged under the local government reorganization.

Village halls have been one of the R.C.C.'s special concerns, because social and recreational pursuits are at the heart of community life. Then follow playing fields, which take a high place in the programme.

Community and development councils come next, aiming at inspired leadership. These community councils have brought a great deal of life to Suffolk. This movement which has been operating for about a dozen years has engendered a tremendous spirit in some 140 towns and villages.

A Suffolk Craft Society has sprung up resulting in twelve practising crafts. Some of the designer-craftsmen are recognized nationally and on the continent of Europe for both creativity in design and high standards of workmanship and skill. Annual exhibitions are usually held at Snape during the period of the Aldeburgh Festival.

Old people's welfare is also included in the sphere of the R.C.C. who hope to provide a laundry service and a night-sitter service. In other words an ever watchful good-neighbour service. It also aims at the creation of day clubs where elderly people can drop in at will.

There is also a public relations service, where letters are received and dealt with. These include a wide range of problems and inquiries from people who wish to return from Australia, to such questions as to how to deal with ants in a bed or obtain a passport.

A Local History Council holds a large place in the scheme of things. This has created a most excellent interest in preserving records of the past for posterity. It has been in existence for about a quarter of a century. This includes a photographic survey with a collection of some 7,000 prints and negatives of old Suffolk, grouped under parishes. It has created a large number of voluntary recorders, so essential in a fast-changing countryside. The L.H.C. is also behind that very ambitious project, the Abbot's Hall Museum of Rural Life, which aims at being a Suffolk Folk Museum, somewhat on the lines of the Netherlands Open Air Museum at Arnhem. Without its aid much of old Suffolk life would have disappeared. One of the most interesting acquisitions was the fourteenth-century farmhouse with its aisled hall, known as Edgar's Farmhouse, from Combs. There is also a seventeenth-century barn from Hill Farm, Grundisburgh. When the Alton Water Reservoir comes into being, the splendid Alton Mill is to be re-erected at Abbot's Hall.

The R.C.C. deals with a Review of Charities, Domestic Food Production, St. John Council for Suffolk; and assists that excellent institution the Suffolk Naturalists' Society. The highlight of 1971, for example, was the record of five birds which had hitherto not been recorded for Suffolk, three of them natives of North America.

But perhaps the most worthy, because of its splendid purpose, is the award of trophies for the Best-kept Village. As a result people have been known to exclaim, "I have never seen the village looking so nice."

When one adds up all these aims and objects, with all the amenities in the way of mod-cons that have come to the village, it is hardly to be wondered that they have become much sought after as places in which to live, particularly if a cottage not so long ago almost condemned can be obtained at a fantastic price. The deserted village has become once again the most populous of the plain.

One is inclined to ask, however, was there ever an era of such cataclysmic change? Not merely in a few or even important ways of life, but in every mortal thing and the smallest detail, even to the extension of one's own life, so that it can be said, "For all that moveth doth in change delight." Disraeli once said, "Change is inevitable. In a progressive country change is constant."

Take for instance shipping. East Suffolk has been always a maritime region with its ports facing the turbulent North Sea, and its sons manning all kinds of sailing vessels that not only plied in local waters but across the oceans of the world. What a noble record belongs to the fishermen, and not least the lifeboatmen who never hung back when the sea was at its worst.

Now comes a revolution in shipping with what is known as cellular ships, handling container and pallet traffic, in a roll-on-roll-off process. Soon the old methods of handling cargoes will be as dead as the coaling stations of the world. Then, continued dock disputes in London and Liverpool have led our own haven ports into sudden prominence, so that Harwich, Felixstowe and

Ipswich will soon be amongst the great European ports. For example more than 2,000 tons of cargo is being moved in each direction between the Polish ports of Gdynia and Ipswich each week. There is also a regular link with West Africa for towns in Liberia and the Ivory Coast. A trade has also sprung up with Piraeus, Famagusta and Beirut, Cyprus and Haifa and Ashdod in Israel.

This has meant a cry for more and more space. In this matter Ipswich is particularly affected, especially when it comes to tank farms for thousands of tons of fuel oil and chemicals. It also means more terminal facilities with huge gantry cranes, high transporter cranes, container cranes. As far as Ipswich is concerned this has been in part solved by reclaiming 50 acres from the oozy west shore of lovely Orwell's bank. In so doing the old Stoke bathing place has been obliterated. It is being done in stages and the first yielded 12 acres and 650 feet of quay for a container berth, a roll-on-roll-off ramp and a transport shed. In a few years' time the quay will probably be extended by 1,300 feet.

The cargoes handled have also seen great changes. Who would imagine that Pilsen beer is made from Suffolk malt shipped from Ipswich. Malt is also sent to the African continent, the Far East and South America. This is taken to the Port of London in R. & W. Paul's four wooden barges for transhipment into ocean-going vessels.

In the old days Suffolk was famous for its maltings, when the barley was spread on floors to germinate. It had to be turned at regular intervals by the manual labour of the malster, using a wooden shove. Their skill and judgement was called on to ensure a satisfactory product. Now it is done by big automatic malting plants and many of the picturesque outlines of the old buildings have gone; but some have been put to use as halls and museums.

An old trade with France, carried on when Dunwich was a port, has been revived by the Societé des Vins de France. They have opened a warehouse on South West Quay, Ipswich, with a bottling plant and a storage capacity of 30,000 gallons. The wine is imported in 550-gallon tanks carried as a deck cargo.

Yet another cargo has been daffodils to Germany—who would have thought it possible? It appears that these flowers, the harbingers of spring, are earlier than in Germany. They are grown in

Lincolnshire and shipped via Ipswich and Holland, as a return load for fresh Dutch produce shipped daily from Maassluis.

We hear so much about Ransomes, Sims and Jefferies in world markets, and particularly of late in establishing themselves in the E.E.C., that we are inclined to forget that their main market is still the United Kingdom. Similarly we are inclined to think of them as connected solely with agricultural machinery, but they are the largest manufacturers in the whole of Britain for counter-balanced battery electric forklift trucks (rather a mouthful). The sales of these trucks amount to a quarter of their turnover and are increasing.

William Pretty and Sons, a 150-year-old firm, is producing nylon fabrics for fashions and household textiles.

Another essentially local product is that of timber shell domes. These curious-looking affairs are springing up in all kinds of places, and take on the appearance of Arctic dwellings. The firm claims that the shape evolves itself like magic. They are built up on a geometrical basis to carry the load consecutively from one piece of material to another by a balance of forces.

Reavell and Co., another old Ipswich name, are producing compressed air plants used in nuclear submarines, as also for the treatment of sewage. While Grain Holdings Ltd. has produced a grain-drier with a nominal capacity of 20 tons per hour. Unfortunately, this has not improved the quality of the loaf—soggy stuff hardly fit to eat—but that is the fault of modern methods of baking. Turner Grain Handling (Ipswich) Ltd. is an offshoot of E. R. and F. Turner Ltd., now no more. It is claimed that Ipswich also holds a top position in the manufacture of cigars.

Industries elsewhere in the county are springing up. Lowestoft, from a fishing port, has become the principal manufacturing centre for north-east Suffolk, particularly in food processing. Shipbuilding by Brooke Marine has won international recognition. Bodies for buses are also made in Lowestoft as well as prams, shoes and artists' materials.

Woodbridge possesses a canning factory, carries on boat-building and the making of electronics, with the manufacture of brushes. While still on the water front is the old tide mill. Eye produces strawboards for building, and has a poultry processing establishment. Martlesham has provided an Office Research

Lowestoft trawler fleet

Station for the Post Office. Brantham on the the Suffolk–Essex border has a large industrial complex making plastics and film base.

Ipswich, once a market town and a centre for agriculture, has been transformed into a semi-industrial town and a great commercial centre. It has been always prosperous because of the diversity of its industries, but some are concerned lest it should lose its identity. The Government rejected its new-town scheme, suggesting that it should expand in its own way. Inevitably, any substantial expansion must take place outside the present boundaries.

In 1971, it was announced that Ipswich was to have a new by-pass, running round the southern side of the town. Opened in 1984, it crosses the Orwell by a high-level bridge and takes traffic from London and the Midlands, via the Ipswich Western By-pass, opened in 1986. Ipswich has been spared ugly motorway architecture: the route from the Midlands is treated as the main thoroughfare with traffic from London and to Lowestoft joining or leaving it by means of slip roads to roundabouts at a different level. Here development has taken place without too much damage. But, as always, how to develop without loss of charm is difficult to imagine.

Dock End Yard is the last of the Ipswich shipyards, and an old man of 72 was called back recently to man a cranse iron for a barge's bowsprit.

Amidst all this amalgam of new industries and inventions, it is good to be able to turn to the old traditional occupations. Thatching still holds its fascination and the demand outstrips the number qualified to accomplish the job. Farriery seems to be on its way back, together with saddlery. Hurdle-making is carried on at Barrow near Bury St. Edmunds, but with modern tools such as an electric drill.

This brings us back to agriculture, the bed-rock of Suffolk stability. British agriculture is as highly mechanized as any in the world. This machinery has been supplied by Ransomes Sims and Jefferies since it first started all those years ago, so that it can announce that more than half its turnover is for agricultural needs. These farming tools include tractors, rotary cultivators, self-propelled harvesters, mechanical handling equipment, sprayers, irrigation equipment, simple tillage tools, seed drills and balers.

The statistics of farm workers is giving rise to great concern, because, although quite a number start, many soon seek other employment because of the lower rate of wage. This means that much of the work is being done by an ageing labour force. If, on the other hand, we have a stagnant economy, another job is not quite so quickly found. Unfortunately these newcomers are apt to treat the work merely as a job and not a career.

Taking East Anglia as a whole, 31 per cent of all farm holdings are still under 20 acres, 38 per cent are under 100 acres, and 23 per cent are under 300 acres, leaving about 8 per cent above the last figure. Taking no account of part-time workers, this means about one regular worker to 60 acres, it also excludes the use of family labour, as there are holdings with no outside labour at all. Thirty years ago there were five workers to each employer, but today employees and employers are almost equal. It might be mentioned that the family farm is still an integral part of E.E.C. agriculture, and resists strongly any effort to be phased out.

A new significance has been introduced into farm labour by the introduction of craftsmen's certificates, which came into force in May 1972. It may well be also that as unemployment in other spheres grows, so work on the land will become a necessity, for there is a startling interdependence of things and conditions in our economy of life.

As it is, Suffolk farming today might be described as in the Golden Bowl era. Wealthy financiers (and there are still people about with vast sums of money in spite of taxmasters), and large investment groups are investing in agricultural land and farms, as a security against inflation. This is a strange situation since one could buy farm land for next to nothing just after the Second World War. Farmers themselves who already have large acreages are also looking for more land, expecting to cash in with higher prices for their produce in the Common Market. Financiers are even disposing of stocks and shares to do this, because when capital gains tax is paid on these shares, it is still worthwhile for major investors to buy land because of the eventual tax benefits and the lower rate of estate duty.

A nightmare picture has been drawn of what Britain (including Suffolk) may be like by the end of the century with 50 million of its 70 million population crowded in an area south-east of the line between the Wash and Bristol. We are bound to have more high-rise buildings simply because horizontal spread will be impossible. There would then be about 40 million cars on the roads. More great swathes would be cut through the countryside and millions more acres would disappear under roads, houses, spaghetti junctions and airports. We may even have skyscraper farms. As factory farming increases we shall not only have intensive animal production like broilers and pigs, but crops in skyscraper plots like gigantic window boxes. What a prospect looms in the not far distance!

One of the duties of our new county council will be to look into the problem of our roads, medieval ways not made for over-weight lorries to rush by unheeding damage caused to old buildings by vibration and in some cases physical contact. It may be that some of this traffic will be diverted back to the railways—which were after all created for the purpose. Instead of closures and the threat of closure this will bring new life to an existing system. The possibility has been demonstrated by the rail terminal at Melton, Woodbridge, by David Allen and Company, as far as the East Suffolk line is concerned.

As Mr. Ernle Money has put it: "The safeguarding of the environment generally remains in the forefront of our national problems, particularly in Suffolk where we have rather more to preserve than perhaps in some other parts of the country."

> Go, songs, for ended is our brief sweet play;
> Go, children of swift joy and tardy sorrow:
> And some are sung, and that was yesterday,
> And some unsung, and that may be to-morrow.
>
> Thompson

Postscript: Suffolk in Prospect

Suffolk became a unified county in 1974, thirteen years ago. It was a prospective change when Allan Jobson wrote *Portrait of Suffolk*. Time has advanced a decade and a half since the original edition.

Suffolk has new challenges beyond the age-old one of creating a prosperous society from growing the grains of bread and beer: the brew of Ipswich is still Cobbolds and Bury still has its Greene King, both of which have been there for several centuries. Suffolk men treat each other with respect and value no man too highly. Wives and husbands talk still in the ageless tongue derived from Old English, not the Middle English of the London dialect which is treated elsewhere as standard.

Yet the county in the last fifteen years has changed. Take transport: there are no trains out to small towns like Hadleigh and Framlingham. Even Lowestoft is at the end of a long branch-line from Ipswich, much of it single track. Paradoxically, north-east Suffolk has become an outpost of the London commuter belt and this trend seems set to continue. The railway line from Norwich to London, through Diss, Stowmarket and Ipswich, is in the process of being turned over to electric traction. In 1987, electric trains already run to Ipswich on an hourly basis from London, and one commuter train goes on to Stowmarket: the railway timetable advises me that it is ninety-four minutes for eighty miles.

The reason is not difficult to see. Inflated salaries in financial markets in the City of London and, for much of the 1970s and early 1980s, low house prices in Suffolk have meant that living two hours from London more than compensates for the pressures of juggling money around.

So far, even Ipswich has been spared the glut of ordinary office workers characteristic of say Margate or Brighton. But it would be no surprise soon to learn of a builder's sales pitch to them with, of course, the attraction of merely a walk to the office from Liverpool Street.

The pull of London is one thing; the pull of Europe is another. In 1973, Britain joined the European Economic Community. Trade across the North Sea increased. To cope with this and the increased importance of the port of Felixstowe, the main road from the Midlands, the A45, was made into a dual carriageway all the way from west of Cambridge. A great by-pass was built round Bury St. Edmunds; another takes both the A45 and the London to Norwich road, the A11, round Newmarket; and there are further roads avoiding Woolpit and Stowmarket. They culminate in the still proceeding boxing-in of Ipswich. A dual carriageway road from the Midlands goes round western Ipswich and then curves south to cross the River Orwell by a high-level bridge.

The Orwell Bridge neatly divides town and country. On the west side there is industry; eastward, the prospect of the river stretches as serenely as it has done for centuries.

There are other new roads in Suffolk. On land that was within the county until 1974, a major industrial estate and trans-shipment centre has been built west of Yarmouth. To give access to it, a new road has been built off the A45 at Bury St. Edmunds, a by-pass has been constructed to take traffic out of Ixworth, and another, in Norfolk, avoids Harleston. There is a new road along the former railway line across Outney Common making a by-pass at Bungay and traffic from Norwich to Lowestoft now does not have to go into Beccles. Other by-passes are planned to avoid Stuston and Thrandeston and doubtless one will be built round Botesdale and the Rickinghalls, two villages still called Inferior and Superior.

Towns and villages have become less traffic-intensive. Much of the centre of Bury St. Edmunds is a pedestrian precinct following the example of Lowestoft. Thanks to the by-passes, the gentleness of Suffolk has returned to its towns: long may it remain.

Suffolk retains, too, its remoteness from the world. A man

can walk along the Suffolk Heritage Coast Path at say Butley or Boyton and look either out to sea or inland and feel a thousand miles from anywhere, with only the cows for company. The same is true on the route of this innovation of the Suffolk County Council to the north in Tunstall Forest or by the Alde marshes, east of Snape. The Walberswick marshes too are without a great influx of 'furriners' and at Reydon Bottom the path, though cut, soon becomes overgrown. There are more people on the coast at the extremities of Bawdsey and Kessingland.

The same remoteness can be felt on the river estuaries: the Deben at Hemley or Waldringfield, the Orwell at Freston or Chelmondiston, the Stour at Arwarton or by Holbrook Bay. However, none of these is more than ten miles from Ipswich.

The land is remote. Walking across fields at Stonham Earl or Gedding, the timelessness of Suffolk remains. It is too precious to be sacrificed to the pressures of the modern world. On Suffolk they obtrude less than elsewhere. Nevertheless there is the persistent ugliness of the air bases at Woodbridge and Bentwaters in the south-east and Mildenhall and Lakenheath in the north-west of the county. There has been the occasional thoughtless demolition in Bury St. Edmunds and the nasty urban dual carriageway there. Ipswich has received a great black box, known from its plan as 'the grand piano': modern architecture at its best or its worst, according to your taste. There is a failed shopping centre there, away from the town centre.

The changed economic world since December 1973 has meant that the traditional Suffolk ability to see beyond tomorrow, the 'selig' of the misnomer "silly Suffolk", has come to the fore. Suffolk, with the wiseness of the 'selig', has turned in on itself, tightened the belt another notch, and watched the 'furriners' with their great lorries take the articulated container transports along the new roads.

The gentle qualities of Suffolk have been writ large in the past decade. Whereas Norfolk exposed a rawness and a harshness born of too long an acquaintance with the sea, Suffolk, with only one face, that of the rising sun, exposed to the sea, has dug deep into its rural roots. The land became less populated: ecclesiastical authorities now worry about the number of village churches serving populations of less than 250, more than a third of all Suffolk villages. With more intensive farming methods, more crops are grown than were a decade ago. Yet the people are fewer.

The need for greater agricultural productivity and a declining rural population has brought a paradox. The shape of the land with the river valleys cutting deep into the core of the county has meant that fields have not been amalgamated to the extent that they have elsewhere. The face of Suffolk has changed less than that of other counties.

Is it, I wonder, the depth of the Suffolk man, the 'selig', which can resist the attraction, if that it be, of the shallow and the simple, the easy solution? Suffolk folk know the hardness of life and have learnt to adapt to its ways. They know it is not easy. They are aware that the clay has to be turned on the morrow. It is surely no accident that the plough-makers, Ransome, Sims and Jefferies, are an Ipswich firm or that Garretts of Leiston developed machinery capable of coping with the basic needs of the farmer.

Allan Jobson began his foreword with a Ransome's plough. I can end this postscript with another, for it is agriculture which has made the Suffolk portrait distinctive.

It is our responsibility to preserve the specialness of Suffolk. It is not part of the affluent south-east, wherever that maybe. It has no need of the shallowness which trifling wealth can convey. Suffolk has a pride all of its own. It transcends money. Suffolk folk know the worth of things and they know, too, that some things are beyond price. Their county above all else.

D.H. Kennett
January 1987

Index

Index